CAMBRIDGE PRIMARY
Mathematics

Challenge

4

Name:

Contents

Emma Low

CAMBRIDGE
UNIVERSITY PRESS

CAMBRIDGE
UNIVERSITY PRESS

University Printing House, Cambridge CB2 8BS, United Kingdom

Cambridge University Press is part of the University of Cambridge.

It furthers the University's mission by disseminating knowledge in the pursuit of education, learning and research at the highest international levels of excellence.

www.cambridge.org
Information on this title: education.cambridge.org/9781316509234

© Cambridge University Press 2016

First published 2016

Printed in Poland by Opolgraf

A catalogue record for this publication is available from the British Library

ISBN 978-1-316-50923-4 Paperback

This book is part of the Cambridge Primary Maths project. This is an innovative combination of curriculum and resources designed to support teachers and learners to succeed in primary mathematics through best-practice international maths teaching and a problem-solving approach.

To get involved, visit
www.cie.org.uk/cambridgeprimarymaths.

Introduction

This *Challenge activity book* is part of a series of 12 write-in activity books for primary mathematics grades 1–6. It can be used as a standalone book, but the content also complements *Cambridge Primary Maths*. Learners progress at different rates, so this series provides a Challenge and Skills Builder activity book for each Primary Mathematics Curriculum Framework Stage to broaden the depth of and to support further learning.

The *Challenge* books extend learning by providing stretching activities to increase the depth of maths knowledge and skills. Support is given through short reminders of key information, topic vocabulary, and hints to prompt learning. These books have been written to support learners whose first language is not English.

How to use the books

The activities are for use by learners in school or at home, with adult support. Topics have been carefully chosen to focus on those areas where learners can stretch their depth of knowledge. The approach is linked directly to *Cambridge Primary Maths*, but teachers and parents can pick and choose which activities to cover, or go through the books in sequence.

The varied set of activities grow in challenge through each unit, including:

- closed questions with answers, so progress can be checked
- questions with more than one possible answer
- activities requiring resources, for example, dice, spinners or digit cards
- activities and games best done with someone else, in class or at home, which give the opportunity for parents and teachers to be fully involved in the child's learning
- activities to support different learning styles: working individually, in pairs, in groups
- a final section of problems and puzzles is provided to challenge learners at the end of Grade 4.

How to approach the activities

Space is provided for learners to write their answers in the book. Some activities might need further practice or writing, so students could be given a blank notebook at the start of the year to use alongside the book. Each activity follows a standard structure.

- **Remember** gives an overview of key learning points. It introduces core concepts and, later, can be used as a revision guide. These sections should be read with an adult who can check that the learner understands the material before attempting the activities.

- **Vocabulary** assists with difficult mathematical terms, particularly when English is not the learner's first language. Learners should read through the key vocabulary. Where necessary, they should be encouraged to clarify their understanding by using a mathematical dictionary or by seeking adult help.

- **Hints** prompt and assist in building understanding, and steer the learner in the right direction.

- **You will need** gives learners, teachers and parents a list of resources for each activity.

- **Photocopiable resources** are provided at the end of the book, for easy assembly in class or at home.

- **Links** to the Cambridge International Examinations Primary Mathematics Curriculum Framework objectives and the corresponding *Cambridge Primary Mathematics Teacher's Resource* are given in the footnote on every page.

- **Calculators** should be used to help learners understand numbers and the number system, including place value and properties of numbers. However, the calculator is not promoted as a calculation tool before Stage 5.

Note:

When a 'spinner' is included, put a paperclip flat on the page so the end is over the centre of the spinner. Place the pencil point in the centre of the spinner, through the paperclip. Hold the pencil firmly and spin the paperclip to generate a result.

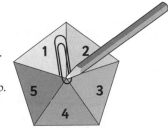

Tracking progress

Answers to closed questions are given at the back of the book – these allow teachers, parents and learners to check their work.

When completing each activity, teachers and parents are advised to encourage self-assessment by asking the students how straightforward they found the activity. When learners are reflecting on games, they should consider how challenging the mathematics was, not who won. Learners could use a ✓/ ✗ or red/ green colouring system to record their self-assessment for each activity.

These assessments provide teachers and parents with an understanding of how best to support individual learners' next steps.

Numbers and the number system

You will need:
resource 1, page 72

Vocabulary
digit, expanded form, partition, place value, thousand

Remember

To solve these problems you need to understand the value of digits in numbers up to 9999, thousands, hundreds, tens and ones. Using this knowledge you can compare and order numbers.

When you multiply a whole number by 10 all of the digits move one place to the left, and 0 is used in the ones place as a place holder.

When you multiply by 100 all of the digits move two places and you need two 0s at the end.

When you divide a number by 10 or 100 the digits move to the right.

1 Shade the expanded form of each number. The first one is done for you.

615, 2370, 5832, 8158, 580

1000	2000	3000	4000	5000	6000	7000	8000	9000
100	200	300	400	500	600	700	800	900
10	20	30	40	50	60	70	80	90
1	2	3	4	5	6	7	8	9

Write down the word that is revealed.

Unit 1A: Number and problem solving
CPM framework 4Nn1, 4Nn3, 4Nn7, 4Nn12, 4Nc15, 4Ps4; Teacher's Resource 1.1, 1.2, 1.3

2 Find your way through the maze. You can only move to a number with greater value than the one you are on.

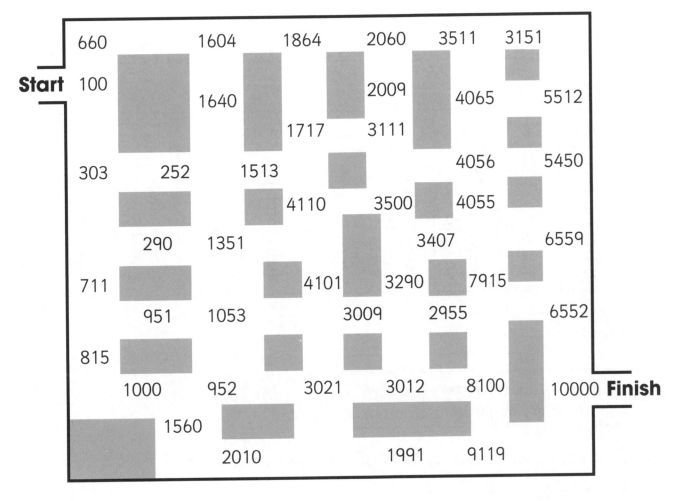

There are at least two routes.
Can you show that you have found every route?

Hint: You can find the dead ends in the maze by identifying numbers that have no greater numbers next to them.

Unit 1A: Number and problem solving
CPM framework 4Nn1, 4Nn3, 4Nn7, 4Nn12, 4Nc15, 4Ps4; Teacher's Resource 1.1, 1.2, 1.3

5

3 Put the numbers in order. Use the code to decipher the word.

8001   1091   811   9080   1000   908   8999   1810

☐ < ☐ < ☐ < ☐ < ☐ < ☐ < ☐ < ☐

Code:

a	e	h	m	n	p	r	s	t	y
$89990 \div 100$	181×10	between 1818 and 1881	between 991 and 1191	$18100 \div 100$	digits total 12	$89990 \div 10$	between 805 and 905	digits total 9	digits total 17

Word = ☐

> **Hint:** Not all the letters are used, and some letters might be used more than once.

4 Find out how numbers up to 10 000 are written in words.

What could this number be?

☐ ☐ N ☐   ☐ ☐ ☐ ☐ ☐ ☐ N ☐

☐ N ☐   ☐ ☐ N ☐ ☐ ☐ ☐   ☐ N ☐

☐ ☐ ☐ ☐ ☐ ☐ ☐ ☐ – ☐ ☐ ☐ ☐ N

I think the number is ☐ .

> **Hint:** Write down the number words. Check how many letters there are in different words and which have the provided letters in them.

Unit 1A: Number and problem solving
CPM framework 4Nn1, 4Nn3, 4Nn7, 4Nn12, 4Nc15, 4Ps4; Teacher's Resource 1.1, 1.2, 1.3

5 A game for two players

Take turns to choose a spinner to spin. Choose to multiply or divide the number shown on the spinner by 10 or 100. If the solution is on the grid, and not already covered, cover it with a counter. The first player to have four counters in a row is the winner.

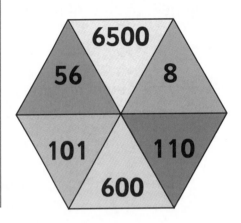

900	65	80	1010
1100	840	4700	6
560	60	650	11
8400	110	90	47

6 Two people are talking about the code to open a safe. Use the clues in the conversation to work out what the four-digit number could be.

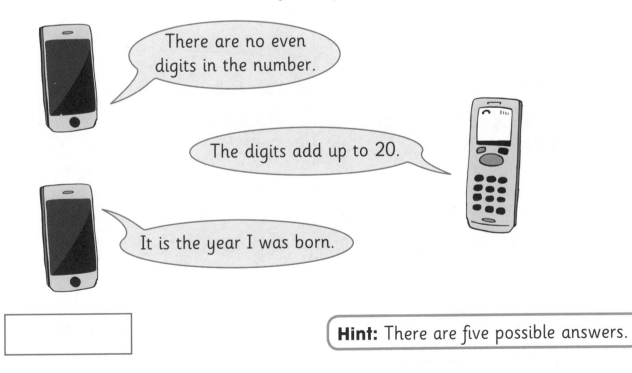

There are no even digits in the number.

The digits add up to 20.

It is the year I was born.

Hint: There are five possible answers.

Unit 1A: Number and problem solving
CPM framework 4Nn1, 4Nn3, 4Nn7, 4Nn12, 4Nc15, 4Ps4; Teacher's Resource 1.1, 1.2, 1.3

Addition and subtraction

Remember

To solve these problems you need to choose appropriate mental or written methods of addition and subtraction. Think about the different strategies you have learnt and try to choose the best ones for each problem.

You can add and subtract larger numbers by partitioning them into hundreds, tens and ones. When adding more than two numbers, find pairs of numbers that total a multiple of 10.

You will need:
resource 2, page 73

Vocabulary
add, addition, plus, increase, sum, total, altogether, subtract, subtraction, take, take away, minus, decrease, fewer, leave, difference

1   What numbers can you make by adding together four consecutive numbers? Try totals up to 80.

Example: $8 + 9 + 10 + 11 = 38$

Think of a way to organise and present your investigation.

Remember to look for pairs of numbers that total 10 or 20.

Do you find anything interesting about the totals that can be made? Try to work out why.

Hint: Consecutive numbers are those that follow on, one after another, in the counting sequence. 8, 9, 10 and 11 are consecutive numbers.

Unit 1A: Number and problem solving
CPM framework 4Nc6, 4Nc9, 4Nc10, 4Nc17, 4Nc18, 4Nc19, 4Ps3, 4Pt1; Teacher's Resource 2.1, 2.2, 2.3

2 Write the correct number on each shirt.

Hint: Start by calculating Alyssa's number, then Kim's number. Read the clues carefully to work out the other numbers.

3 Enter the maze and make your way to the centre. Add on each number that you go through. Try to reach 200 with a total of 200.
Record your addition calculations here.

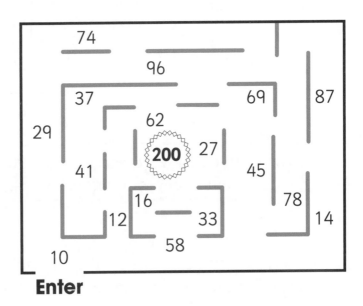

Hint: Try to use quick mental methods to add the two numbers. Think about how you can apply your strategies for adding two-digit numbers quickly to adding a two-digit number to a number between 100 and 200.

Unit 1A: Number and problem solving
CPM framework 4Nc6, 4Nc9, 4Nc10, 4Nc17, 4Nc18, 4Nc19, 4Ps3, 4Pt1; Teacher's Resource 2.1, 2.2, 2.3

9

4 A game for two players

Use a set of 1 to 30 number cards from resource 2.

Shuffle the cards and place them face down in a pile.

Turn over the top card.

Look for two numbers on the grid with a difference of the number on the card.

The first person to point to it takes the card.

Continue to turn over cards and find the differences between numbers on the grid.

If neither player can find a pair of numbers with the difference that matches the number on the card, place that card at the bottom of the pack.

The first player to have five cards wins the game.

67	28	41	16	33	25	48
81	57	39	27	61	54	45

Hint: All of the differences on the cards can be made, but some can only be made one way and some can be made up to four different ways.

Discuss with your partner the strategies you used for trying to find the correct pair of numbers.

Play the game again, trying to use different strategies to identify the pairs of numbers more quickly.

Unit 1A: Number and problem solving
CPM framework 4Nc6, 4Nc9, 4Nc10, 4Nc17, 4Nc18, 4Nc19, 4Ps3, 4Pt1; Teacher's Resource 2.1, 2.2, 2.3

5 Six friends from wet places around the world have collected rainwater for two weeks.

Abigail collected 476 ml in the first week and 764 ml in the second week. How much water did she collect altogether?

Complete the table with the missing amounts.

Name	Week one (ml)	Week two (ml)	Total (ml)
Abigail	476	764	
Maria	816	396	
Kyle	519		748
Oshi	383		842
Lila		649	1059
Rani		243	1068

Hint: Partition the numbers, and check that each answer is reasonable.
Think of 1000 as 10 hundreds.

What is the difference between the total amounts collected by Kyle and Oshi?

6 Use the digits 4, 5, 6, 7, 8, 9 only once in each calculation to make number sentences that are true.

☐☐☐ − ☐☐☐ = 333

☐☐☐ − ☐☐☐ = 111

☐☐☐ − ☐☐☐ = 273

☐☐☐ − ☐☐☐ = 75

☐☐☐ − ☐☐☐ = 91

☐☐☐ − ☐☐☐ = 327

☐☐☐ − ☐☐☐ = 87

☐☐☐ − ☐☐☐ = 69

Hint: All of the answers are possible, but there are lots of combinations. Choose hundreds values that give a reasonable estimate. Think which pair of digits can go in the ones places to give the correct digit in the ones place of the difference.

Unit 1A: Number and problem solving
CPM framework 4Nc6, 4Nc9, 4Nc10, 4Nc17, 4Nc18, 4Nc19, 4Ps3, 4Pt1; Teacher's Resource 2.1, 2.2, 2.3

Multiplication and division

1   Yousef is paid $13 on the first day.

Each day his pay is double what it was the day before.

Naser is paid $79 every day.

How much has each earned at the end of five days?

Yousef has earned ⬚ .

Hint: When you get above 100, try to apply what you know about doubling two-digit numbers to the three-digit number. Remember that all the days' earnings must be added together to make the total for five days.

Naser has earned ⬚ .

Hint: Use a multiplication method that you know, such as the grid method, to work out how much Naser has earned.

Unit 1A: Number and problem solving
CPM framework 4Nc5, 4Nc13, 4Nc14, 4Nc20, 4Nc21, 4Nc22, 4Nc23, 4Nn8 ,4Ps6, 4Pt6; Teacher's Resource 3.1, 3.2, 3.3

2. The numbers 1 to 10 on this times table grid are not in the usual order along the top and the side. Use the numbers in the grid to work out the correct order. Then fill in the spaces in the grid.

×										
		18		36			54			
	100				30		80			
18			14			6				
	70				35					7
			28				24			4
45		10			25					
				12		9		24		
	60		42							6
		16			40		48			
	9			4				8		

Hint: Use what you know about multiples of 2, 3, 4, 5, and 10 to work out which times table could be in each row or column.

3. Write the 27 times table up to 27 × 10.

☐ , ☐ , ☐ , ☐ , ☐ , ☐ , ☐ , ☐ , ☐ , ☐

Look at the numbers, and the pattern of the numbers, in the 27 times table. What do you notice about the 27 times table?

Choose your own two-digit number and work out its times table.

☐ , ☐ , ☐ , ☐ , ☐ , ☐ , ☐ , ☐ , ☐ , ☐

Do you notice anything about the numbers, and the pattern of the numbers in your times table?

Hint: Use a method of multiplication that you know, such as the grid method, to work out each number in the times tables.

CPM framework 4Nc4, 4Nc5, 4Nc13, 4Nc14, 4Nc20, 4Nc21, 4Nc22, 4Nc23, 4Nn8 ,4Ps6, 4Pt6; Teacher's Resource 3.1, 3.2, 3.3

4 Some pairs of two-digit and one-digit numbers can be multiplied together to give a product of 84, for example, 84 × 1 = 84.

Find five more pairs.

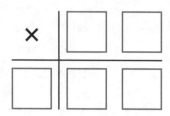

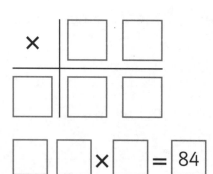

> **Hint:** Think about which times tables 84 could be in.
> Use your knowledge of times tables.
> Be systematic. First try some possible calculations and then get closer to the target of 84 by adjusting one of the numbers.

Unit 1A: Number and problem solving
CPM framework 4Nc5, 4Nc13, 4Nc14, 4Nc20, 4Nc21, 4Nc22, 4Nc23, 4Nn8, 4Ps6, 4Pt6; Teacher's Resource 3.1, 3.2, 3.3

5 To reach the celebration you must start from A, B, C or D and only move horizontally or vertically to numbers that are multiples of 4.

Which letter leads to the celebration? ☐

A	4	16	12	32	2	38	6	34	36	8	20	10	24	40	30	28	B
28	14	26	18	4	22	16	32	16	20	2	36	42	6	4	38	24	10
8	12	40	34	24	14	8	30	18	26	22	12	42	2	16	36	4	38
6	34	16	28	20	4	12	40	32	20	10	30	14	26	18	22	8	40
4	42	2	38	6	34	20	10	14	30	26	24	32	40	2	38	18	24
32	8	6	36	12	28	22	8			38	16	6	4	12	8	42	20
10	24	14	40	30	4	36	6			22	8	2	34	26	16	10	32
34	12	18	28	22	34	16	40	38	24	20	40	42	2	36	24	6	4
10	36	14	8	18	32	12	22	34	26	14	2	10	14	16	2	28	16
20	40	38	4	10	36	34	14	30	8	16	32	4	40	20	18	8	22
8	26	34	32	2	12	28	16	22	2	28	10	6	22	26	30	24	20
C	32	40	4	30	6	26	36	8	32	12	4	28	34	16	20	12	D

Hint: Lightly shade the boxes you pass through, in different colours, to record the ways you have tried.

Unit 1A: Number and problem solving
CPM framework 4Nc5, 4Nc13, 4Nc14, 4Nc20, 4Nc21, 4Nc22, 4Nc23, 4Nn8, 4Ps6, 4Pt6; Teacher's Resource 3.1, 3.2, 3.3

6 Tick the numbers that you can make from 1 to 20 by completing each division sentence.
Put a cross next to those you cannot make.

Only use these digits. The same digit must not appear more than once in each division sentence.

> **Hint:** You can use multiplication as the inverse of division.

1 2 3 4 5 6 7 8 9

☐ ☐ ÷ ☐ = 1   ☐ ☐ ÷ ☐ = 11

☐ ☐ ÷ ☐ = 2   ☐ ☐ ÷ ☐ = 12

☐ ☐ ÷ ☐ = 3   ☐ ☐ ÷ ☐ = 13

☐ ☐ ÷ ☐ = 4   ☐ ☐ ÷ ☐ = 14

☐ ☐ ÷ ☐ = 5   ☐ ☐ ÷ ☐ = 15

☐ ☐ ÷ ☐ = 6   ☐ ☐ ÷ ☐ = 16

☐ ☐ ÷ ☐ = 7   ☐ ☐ ÷ ☐ = 17

☐ ☐ ÷ ☐ = 8   ☐ ☐ ÷ ☐ = 18

☐ ☐ ÷ ☐ = 9   ☐ ☐ ÷ ☐ = 19

☐ ☐ ÷ ☐ = 10   ☐ ☐ ÷ ☐ = 20

Unit 1A: Number and problem solving
CPM framework 4Nc5, 4Nc13, 4Nc14, 4Nc20, 4Nc21, 4Nc22, 4Nc23, 4Nn8, 4Ps6, 4Pt6; Teacher's Resource 3.1, 3.2, 3.3

Weight

You will need: bags, classroom objects, weighing scales

Remember

To solve these problems you need to know that 1 kg = 1000 g.

Vocabulary
approximate, gram, kilogram

1 Order the parcels from the lightest to the heaviest.

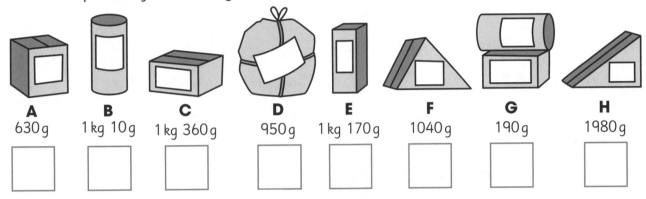

A	**B**	**C**	**D**	**E**	**F**	**G**	**H**
630 g	1 kg 10 g	1 kg 360 g	950 g	1 kg 170 g	1040 g	190 g	1980 g

Mark each weight on the scale as accurately as you can.

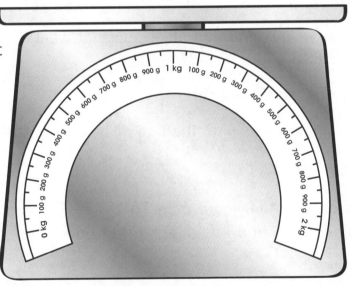

Hint: You could find the lightest parcel and cross it out, then find the next lightest, and so on.

2 The same parcel was placed on four different weighing scales. Label the scales with multiples of 100 to make them correct.

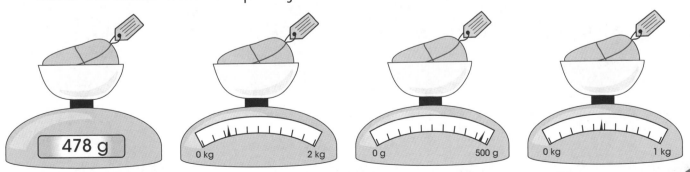

478 g

0 kg   2 kg   0 g   500 g   0 kg   1 kg

3 Add objects to a bag or box until it weighs your estimate of 100 g.

Weigh the bag. Record the weight. [ ] g

Remove, add or swap items until the bag or box weighs 100 g.

Hint: Each time you try to estimate the weight of a new bag and objects, compare it to the previous bag. It should be double the weight.

Take another bag or box and add objects until it weighs your estimate of 200 g.

Weigh the bag. Record the weight. [ ] g

Remove, add or swap items until the bag or box weighs 200 g.

Take another bag or box and add objects until it weighs your estimate of 400 g.

Weigh the bag. Record the weight. [ ] g

Remove, add or swap items until the bag or box weighs 400 g.

Take another bag or box and add objects until it weighs your estimate of 800 g.

Weigh the bag. Record the weight. [ ] g

Remove, add or swap items until the bag or box weighs 800 g.

4 Postal workers must not lift more than 16 kg.
Arrange these packages into two piles so that both piles can be lifted safely.

A	B	C	D	E	F
3100 g	4900 g	3950 g	7200 g	3700 g	8900 g

Unit 1B: Measure and problem solving
CPM framework 4MI1, 4MI2, 4MI4, 4Pt2; Teacher's Resource 4.1

5

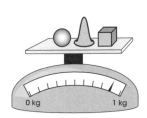  

How much does one cone weigh? ☐

How much does one cube weigh? ☐

How much does one sphere weigh? ○ ☐

Draw on the scale how much this group of objects would weigh.

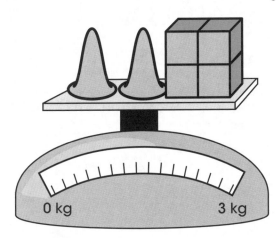

> **Hint:** Try different values for the cone, sphere and cube until all of the balance scales are correct. Think how you will record the values you have tried and decide which to try next.

6 Most adults weigh between 50 kg and 100 kg.

If an elevator can safely hold a maximum of 1250 kg, what would be the maximum number of adults you would allow in an elevator? ☐

Explain how you worked out your answer.

> **Hint:** There is more than one reasonable answer. Explain why your answer is safe but allows as many people as possible to use the elevator at one time.

Pictograms

Remember

To solve these problems you need to understand how symbols and a key are used to represent more than one item in a pictogram.

Vocabulary

pictogram

1 This pictogram shows some people's favourite genres of films.

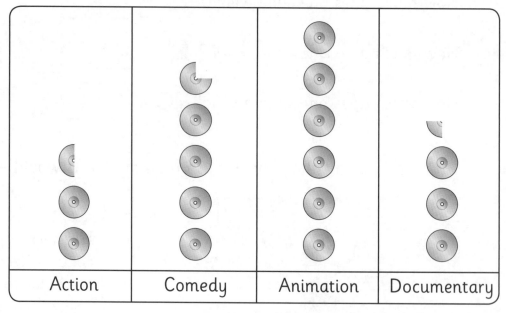

| Action | Comedy | Animation | Documentary |

Which is the most popular?

Which is the least popular?

The pictogram represents 330 people in total.

Complete the key. ⊙ = people.

Complete the table to match the pictogram.

Film genre	Number of people
Action	
Comedy	
Animation	
Documentary	

Hint: Estimate a number of people that one symbol could represent. Try that number in the pictogram to see if all the symbols total 330.

Unit 1C: Handling data and problem solving,
CPM framework 4Dh1, 4Pt8; Teacher's Resource 7.12

2 Leo, Bruno, Jamil and Vijay collect stickers.

Use the clues to complete the pictogram showing how many stickers each of them has collected.

Clues

Leo has three fewer stickers than Bruno.

In total they all have 169 stickers.

Jamil has 10 fewer stickers than Vijay.

Bruno has 44 stickers.

Key ⭐ = 5 stickers

Pictogram

3 Convert the information in the table into a pictogram.

Remember to include a title, labels and a key.

Hint: Look carefully at the data before choosing a scale and a symbol for your key.

Destinations of aeroplanes leaving the airport in a week	
Destination	**Number of flights**
Rome	140
Tokyo	40
Ottawa	55
Rio de Janeiro	10
Nairobi	20

Carroll and Venn diagrams

Remember

To solve these problems you need to understand how Carroll and Venn diagrams are used to sort data. Read the headings and labels carefully to see how and where items should be sorted.

You will need: resource 1, page 72 for activity 1, coloured pencils or pens

Vocabulary
sort, classify, Carroll diagram, Venn diagram

1 Use these digits in the number sentences so that one answer can be placed into each section of the Carroll diagram on resource 1. You may use each digit only once.

| 2 | 3 | 4 | 5 | 6 | 7 | 8 | 9 |

☐ + ☐ = ☐   ☐ × ☐ = ☐

☐ − ☐ = ☐   ☐ ÷ ☐ = ☐

Hint: Think about numbers that are multiples of both 3 and 4. Think which numbers give a whole number when divided.

2 These children are sitting on a bus as if they are part of a Carroll diagram.

Add these labels to the picture.

| Hat | No hat | Tie | No tie |

Work out who is sitting where.
Label the picture with their names.

Albert: I am not wearing a hat.

Adam: I am not sitting next to Amos.

Archie: I am wearing a tie and a hat.

Amos: I am not wearing a tie.

Unit 1C: Handling data and problem solving
CPM framework objectives 4Dh3, 4Ps4; Teacher's Resource 8.1, 8.2

3 Draw a flower for each section of the Venn diagram.

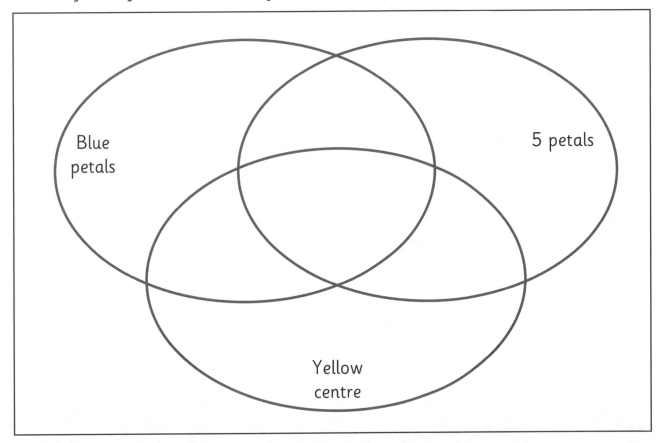

> **Hint:** Remember to draw a flower in the section outside of the loops.

4 20 children are performing in a singing and dancing show.

15 children are singing and 8 children are dancing.

How many children are singing and dancing?

Use the Venn diagram to help you solve the problem.

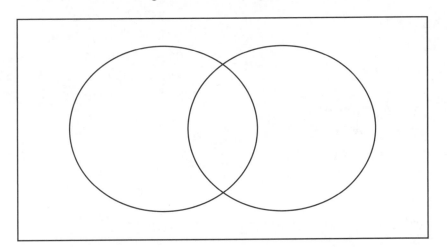

> **Hint:** Write numbers in the sections that make all of the statements true.

Place value and decimals in context

Remember

To solve these problems you need to understand that the position of any digit in a number tells you its value. Some of the positions are tens, ones, tenths and hundredths.

You can round numbers to the nearest multiple of 1, 10, 100, ... If a number is halfway between two multiples, then always round up.

You will need:
a place-value chart from resource 1, page 72

Vocabulary
tenth, hundredth, place value

1 Who will reach over 5000 first if they start at the same time and count at the same speed?

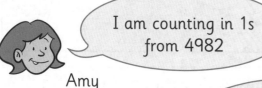

I am counting in 1s from 4982

Amy

I am counting in 10s from 4838

Ali

I am counting in 100s from 3089

Aadi

Who will reach under 5000 first if they start at the same time and count at the same speed?

I am counting backwards in 100s from 6907

Amy

I am counting backwards in 1s from 5024

Ali

I am counting backwards in 10s from 5183

Aadi

Hint: Choose a way to count the numbers that each child will say.

Unit 2A: Measure and problem solving
CPM framework 4Nn2, 4Nn3, 4Nn4, 4Nn9, 4Ps4; Teacher's Resource 9.1

2 Use these digits to make a number that gives 7300 when rounded to the nearest 100.

| 2 | 3 | 5 | 7 |

| |

Use these digits to make a number that gives 4010 when rounded to the nearest 10.

| 0 | 1 | 3 | 4 |

| |

3 Partition these amounts of money into tens, ones, tenths and hundredths. Shade each part of each amount on the grid.

| $17.25 | $75.80 | $90.00 | $39.50 |

| $20.02 | $52.70 | $80.97 |

10	20	30	40	50	60	70	80	90
1	2	3	4	5	6	7	8	9
0.1	0.2	0.3	0.4	0.5	0.6	0.7	0.8	0.9
0.01	0.02	0.03	0.04	0.05	0.06	0.07	0.08	0.09

What word do the shaded parts reveal? | |

4 Work out which purse belongs to which child.
How much money does each child have?

$5.50 $4.79 $9.75 $7.94 $6.50

Maria: I have more money than Josie.

Caleb: My money rounds to $5, to the nearest dollar.

Tansy: The tenths digit in my amount of money is 9.

Ahmed: I have the most money.

Josie: My money rounds to $6, to the nearest dollar.

5 Samir, Greta and Lila have been collecting cents in jars.

Samir 539   **Samir 369**   **Greta 607**   **Greta 373**   **Lila 478**   **Lila 135**   **Lila 286**

How much has each person collected? Give your answer in dollars.

Samir [   ]   Greta [   ]   Lila [   ]

Who collected the least money? [   ]

Who collected the most money? [   ]

Hint: When you are adding three numbers, add two of the numbers first then add on the other number.

Unit 2A: Measure and problem solving
CPM framework 4Nn2, 4Nn3, 4Nn4, 4Nn9, 4Ps4; Teacher's Resource 9.1

6 Mark the approximate positions of these amounts on the money number line.

$1	150 cents
$0.50	$1.95
27 cents	$0.06
$1.08	$0.81
118 cents	$1.88
$1.32	62 cents

Hint: Convert numbers of cents into dollars first.

$2

$0

Unit 2A: Measure and problem solving
CPM framework 4Nn2, 4Nn3, 4Nn4, 4Nn9, 4Ps4; Teacher's Resource 9.1

Odd, even and negative numbers

Remember

To solve these problems you need to understand what happens when you find the sum of pairs of odd and even numbers and some of the properties of odd and even numbers.

< is the symbol for **less than**, > is the symbol for **greater than**.

You can draw a number line with numbers lower than zero to help you solve problems involving negative and positive numbers.

1 Use each number once to make these statements correct.

| −13 | −4 | 7 | −17 | 5 | 12 | −3 |

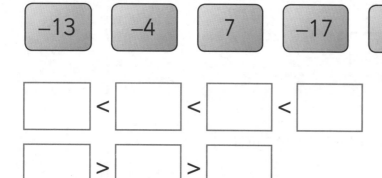

Find another solution to the problem.

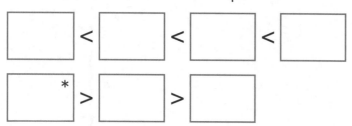

Which of the numbers cannot go in the box marked with a star *?

Unit 2A: Number and problem solving
CPM framework 4Nn13, 4Nn14, 4Nn15, 4Nn16, 4Pt8; Teacher's Resource 9.2, 9.3

2 Thermometer code

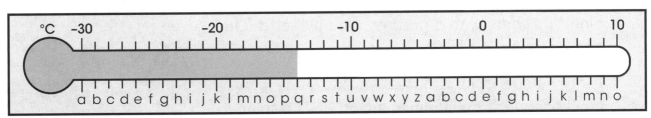

Solve the clues and use the code on the thermometer to work out the secret word.

Clues

10 degrees higher than –6°C [ ]

5 degrees lower than 3°C [ ]

20 degrees lower than –2°C [ ]

8 degrees lower than –20°C [ ]

20 degrees lower than 1°C [ ]

16 degrees higher than –16°C [ ]

12 degrees higher than –24°C [ ]

The word is [ ]

Hint: Use the thermometer as a number line to help you solve the clues.

---

3 Start at A, B, C or D. Follow the left arrow at odd numbers, follow the right arrow at even numbers. Does the path from A, B, C or D get to the goal?

← → 2003	↑	← → 6741	Goal			← → 6727	↑	← → 9487
↑	← → 9528	↑	← → 3447		← → 708	↑	← → 6225	↑
← → 782	↑	← → 5283	↑	← → 829	↑	← → 8210	↑	← → 8181
↑	← → 8213	↑	← → 8382	↑	← → 6005	↑	← → 7010	↑
← → 6331	↑	← → 2851	↑	← → 9284	↑	← → 9928	↑	← → 9881
↑	← → 4772	↑	← → 358	↑	← → 7314	↑	← → 228	↑
← → 1374	↑	← → 8207	↑	← → 5563	↑	← → 1881	↑	← → 713
↑	← → 819	↑	← → 5185	↑	← → 9781	↑	← → 2293	↑
← → 7986	↑	← → 8329	↑	← → 3083	↑	← → 4827	↑	← → 6489
↑	← → 1891	↑	← → 502	↑	← → 8416	↑	← → 3456	↑
	A		**B**		**C**		**D**	

Unit 2A: Number and problem solving
CPM framework 4Nn13, 4Nn14, 4Nn15, 4Nn16, 4Pt8; Teacher's Resource 9.2, 9.3

4   Odds and evens spinner game

Play this game with a partner. One player is 'Odds' and one player is 'Evens'.

If the number spun is odd, then the 'Odds' player moves forward the number shown on the spinner. If it is even then the 'Evens' player moves forward the number shown on the spinner.

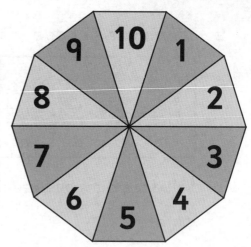

The first player to reach the finish or beyond is the winner.

Is the game fair? | yes / no |

Explain your answer.

Unit 2A: Number and problem solving
CPM framework 4Nn13, 4Nn14, 4Nn15, 4Nn16, 4Pt8; Teacher's Resource 9.2, 9.3

Cheng and Raphael are playing the game.
Which one of these boards shows where their counters were part way through the game?

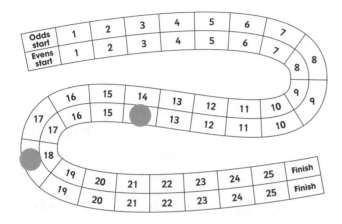

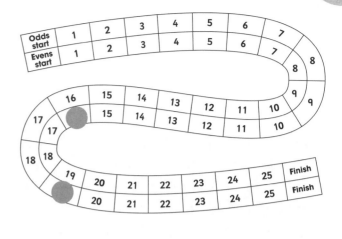

How do you know?

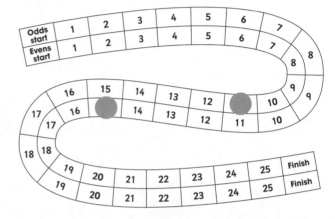

Hint: Think about which of the numbers on the spinner are odd and which are even.

5   Without working out the answers can you tell whether the answers to these calculations are odd or even?

8706 + 19498

77319 + 688428

842231 + 96807

743595 × 2

11849 × 10

1 + 12 + 123 + 1234 + 12345

Hint: The number of digits in a number makes no difference to whether it is odd or even.

Addition, subtraction, multiplication and division

Remember

You know different mental and written methods to add, subtract, multiply and divide. Look at the numbers and choose the most efficient method for each calculation.

You can use the inverse to check your answers. Addition is the inverse of subtraction. Multiplication is the inverse of division.

You will need:
counters in 2 colours, 2 paperclips, a pencil or pin to use the spinners

Vocabulary
add, addition, sum, total, subtraction, subtraction, difference, multiply, multiplication, product, divide, division, quotient

1   What is the closest total to 800 you can make with two of these numbers?

789	503	402	605
197	901	899	395

What is the closest difference to 300 you can make with two of these numbers?

Hint: All of these numbers are near multiples of 100.

Unit 2A: Number and problem solving
CPM framework 4Nc18, 4Nn6, 4Nc8, 4Nc9, 4Nc10, 4Nc11, 4Nc12, 4Nc22, 4Nc23, 4Nc4, 4Nc5, 4Nc13, 4Nc14, 4Nc16, 4Ps3, 4Pt1, 4Pt6;
Teacher's Resource 10.1, 10.2, 11.1, 11.2

2 Play this game with a partner.

Take turns to use both spinners to select two numbers.
Subtract the smaller number from the larger number.

Cover your solution on this grid with a counter, if it is not already covered.

The first player to cover three numbers in a row, vertically, horizontally or diagonally, is the winner.

399	398	397	396	395	394
393	392	391	390	389	388
299	298	297	296	295	294
293	292	291	290	289	288

Which four numbers in the grid cannot be made by subtracting the numbers on the spinners?

Hint: Think about whether a mental or written method is more efficient for these calculations.

Unit 2A: Number and problem solving

CPM framework 4Nc18, 4Nn6, 4Nc8, 4Nc9, 4Nc10, 4Nc11, 4Nc12, 4Nc22, 4Nc23, 4Nc4, 4Nc5, 4Nc13, 4Nc14, 4Nc16, 4Ps3, 4Pt1, 4Pt6;
Teacher's Resource 10.1, 10.2, 11.1, 11.2

33

3 Use these three digits to make the number sentence true.

$$\boxed{} \times \boxed{}\boxed{} = 63$$

Use these three digits to make the number sentence true.

$$\boxed{} \times \boxed{}\boxed{} = 230$$

Use these three digits to make the number sentence true.

$$\boxed{} \times \boxed{}\boxed{} = 686$$

4 Find numbers less than 10 that divide into 97 leaving the remainder 1, 2, 6, and 7.

$$97 \div \boxed{} = \boxed{} \text{ remainder } 1$$

$$97 \div \boxed{} = \boxed{} \text{ remainder } 2$$

$$97 \div \boxed{} = \boxed{} \text{ remainder } 6$$

$$97 \div \boxed{} = \boxed{} \text{ remainder } 7$$

Find all the possible numbers up to 10 that give the remainder 1.

Hint: You could work systematically through the numbers from 2 to 9, or you could start by using what you know about the numbers in some times tables.

Unit 2A: Number and problem solving
CPM framework 4Nc18, 4Nn6, 4Nc8, 4Nc9, 4Nc10, 4Nc11, 4Nc12, 4Nc22, 4Nc23, 4Nc4, 4Nc5, 4Nc13, 4Nc14, 4Nc16, 4Ps3, 4Pt1, 4Pt6;
Teacher's Resource 10.1, 10.2, 11.1, 11.2

5 Write all of the one-digit and two-digit numbers in which the sum of the digits equals 9, e.g. 36, 3 + 6 = 9.

Put them in order, from smallest to largest.

What number pattern have you made?

6 Each of these children started with a two-digit number, they doubled it then doubled again. Work out their starting numbers.

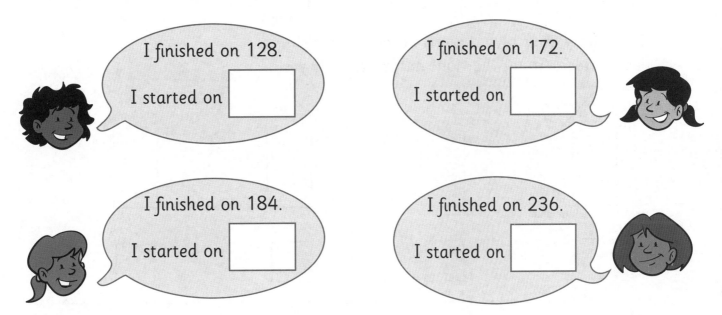

I finished on 128.

I started on

I finished on 172.

I started on

I finished on 184.

I started on

I finished on 236.

I started on

Hint: Halving is the inverse of doubling.

Unit 2A: Number and problem solving

CPM framework 4Nc18, 4Nn6, 4Nc8, 4Nc9, 4Nc10, 4Nc11, 4Nc12, 4Nc22, 4Nc23, 4Nc4, 4Nc5, 4Nc13, 4Nc14, 4Nc16, 4Ps3, 4Pt1, 4Pt6;
Teacher's Resource 10.1, 10.2, 11.1, 11.2

35

Angles, position and direction

You will need: a ruler, scissors, tracing paper

Remember

You can record a position on a grid by how far it is along the horizontal axis first, then how far it is up or down the vertical axis.

A right angle is 90°. A full turn is 360°.

Vocabulary
right angle, ordered pair, axis

1 Tan has made this design by adding straight lines to the 12-sided shape.

How many right angles does each stage of his design have?

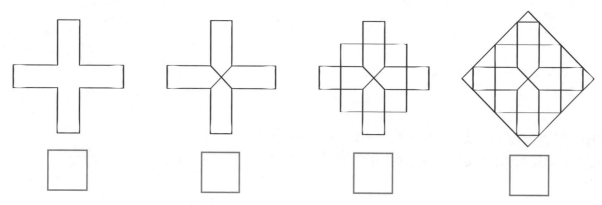

Now draw your own designs based on this shape.
Use a ruler. Count the right angles in each design.

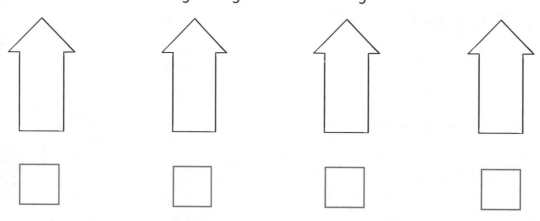

Hint: Use a right-angle checker to check whether an angle is a right angle.
You can make a right-angle checker by taking a circle of paper and folding it neatly into quarters. The angle where the two folded edges meet is a right angle.

Unit 2B: Geometry and problem solving, 12.1 Angles and turning, 12.2 Position and direction;
CPM framework objectives 4Gp1, 4Gp2, 4Gp3

2 Find the letters at these positions on the grid.

(H, 4) ☐ (D, 6) ☐

(C, 1) ☐ (A, 3) ☐

(E, 2) ☐ (E, 5) ☐

(G, 7) ☐

Rearrange the letters to make the name of a shape.

_____

	A	B	C	D	E	F	G	H
8	a	b	c	d	e	f	g	h
7	i	j	k	l	m	n	o	p
6	q	r	s	t	u	v	w	x
5	y	z	a	b	c	d	e	f
4	g	h	i	j	k	l	m	n
3	o	p	q	r	s	t	u	v
2	w	x	y	z	a	b	c	d
1	e	f	g	h	i	j	k	l

3 All of these angles are very close to a right angle, but none of them is exactly 90°. Order them from the smallest to the widest angle.

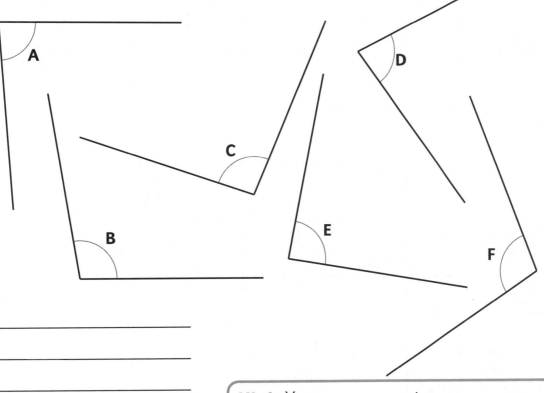

_____

_____

_____

_____

Hint: You can use tracing paper to compare angles that are close in size. Trace one angle onto the tracing paper. Place the traced angle over the other angle to see which is wider.

Unit 2B: Geometry and problem solving, 12.1 Angles and turning, 12.2 Position and direction; CPM framework objectives 4Gp1, 4Gp2, 4Gp3

37

4 Kim started from a shaded square a, b or c, facing north.
She followed the directions and finished at X.
What is the ordered pair of the square where she started?

Forward 2 squares. Turn 90° clockwise.

Forward 3 squares. Turn 180° anticlockwise.

Forward 1 square. Turn 90° clockwise.

Forward 3 squares. Turn 360° clockwise.

Forward 1 square. Turn 90° clockwise.

Forward 2 squares. Turn 90° clockwise.

Forward 2 squares. Turn 90° anticlockwise.

Forward 1 square.

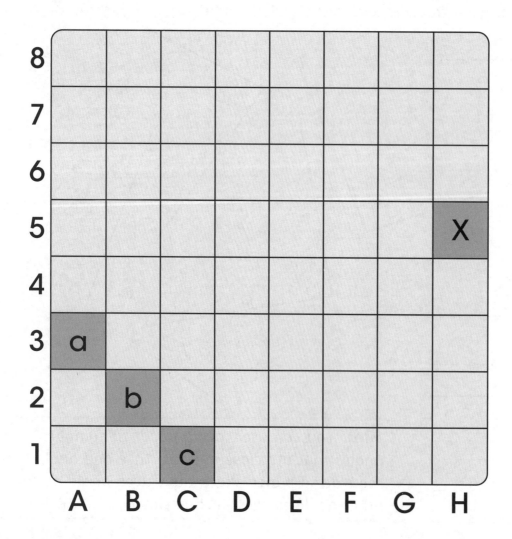

Unit 2B: Geometry and problem solving, 12.1 Angles and turning, 12.2 Position and direction;
CPM framework objectives 4Gp1, 4Gp2, 4Gp3

5 Tom also finished at X. He did not start from a, b or c, but he was facing north. He followed these instructions. Where did he start on the grid?

Forward 1 square. Turn 90° clockwise.

Forward 1 square. Turn 90° clockwise.

Forward 4 squares. Turn 90° clockwise.

Forward 2 squares. Turn 90° anticlockwise.

Forward 3 squares. Turn 90° anticlockwise.

Forward 5 squares. Turn 90° anticlockwise.

Forward 2 squares. Turn 90° clockwise.

Forward 2 squares. Turn 90° anticlockwise.

Forward 2 squares.

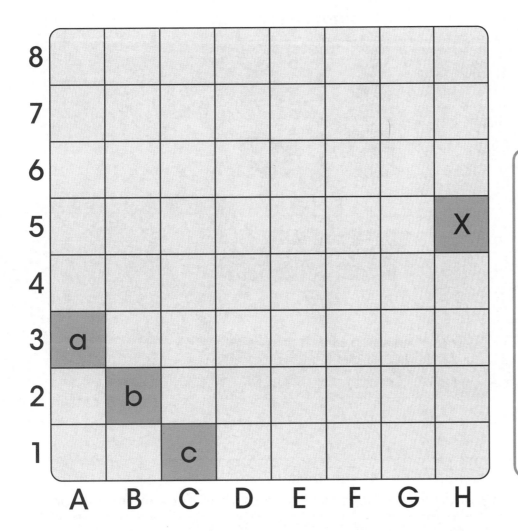

Hint: Use the arrow on the compass to find out which way Kim and Tom were facing at the start of their journeys.
Try working back from X. Work out where Tom must have come from before each instruction.

Unit 2B: Geometry and problem solving, 12.1 Angles and turning, 12.2 Position and direction;
CPM framework objectives 4Gp1, 4Gp2, 4Gp3

Symmetry

You will need: a ruler, scissors, glue, large and small sheets of paper, a small mirror

Remember

To solve these problems you need to understand that shapes and patterns can have reflective symmetry. This means a mirror can be placed on a line through the shape or pattern and it will recreate the rest of the shape or pattern exactly. There can be more than one line of symmetry in a shape or pattern.

Vocabulary
symmetrical, reflective symmetry, mirror line

1 Spot the difference.

Draw shapes on the right side of the picture to make it a reflection of the picture on the left along the mirror line.

Hint: Place a small mirror on the mirror line.
Check that the second picture looks the same as the image in the mirror.

Unit 2B: Geometry and problem solving
CPM framework 4Gs3, 4Gs5, 4Ps7; Teacher's Resource 13.1

2 Copy this table onto a large sheet of paper.
Fold a small piece paper in half in one direction, then again in the other direction.

Cut out a shape at the corner where the folds meet.

Unfold the cut-out shape.

Make more shapes in the same way.

Lines of symmetry			
0	**1**	**2**	**more than 2**

Sort the shapes into those with 0, 1, 2, or more than 2 lines of symmetry and stick them into the table you have drawn.

Try to make at least one shape for each section.

Discuss with a partner whether there are any sections of the table that you cannot make a shape for in this way.

3 These tiles have reflective symmetry in their shape and in their patterns. Mark the mirror lines onto the patterns. Use a ruler.

Hint: Use a small mirror to check the lines of symmetry.

4 Which squares will be shaded when the shape is reflected over the mirror line? Write the ordered pairs.

Hint: Try to visualise and predict which squares will be shaded.

Unit 2B: Geometry and problem solving
CPM framework 4Gs3, 4Gs5, 4Ps7; Teacher's Resource 13.1

2D shapes

You will need: a ruler, pegboard, a small mirror, dotted paper

Remember

To solve these problems you need to know the names and properties of some 2D shapes.
Look up any shape words that you do not know to find out the properties of that shape.
Always use a ruler to draw these shapes.

Vocabulary
quadrilateral, polygon, regular polygon, parallel, parallelogram, pentagon, hexagon, heptagon, octagon

1 Circle all the shapes that are types of parallelogram.

Example:
This is a parallelogram.

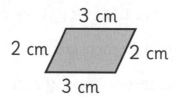

3 cm

2 cm 2 cm

3 cm

Hint: First check that the shape is a quadrilateral. You can measure and record the lengths of each side with a ruler.

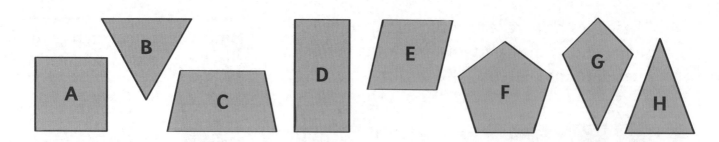

2 Use the ordered pairs to locate dots on the grid.

Visualise the shape that will be made by joining the dots together.

Shape 1: (A, 4), (A, 2), (D, 2), (D, 4)

Shape 2: (C, 2), (B, 3), (C, 4), (D, 3)

Shape 3: (B, 1), (A, 2), (A, 4), (C, 5), (E, 4), (E, 2), (D, 1)

Hint: To check your visualisation you can draw the lines lightly between the dots with a pencil and ruler.

Unit 2B: Geometry and problem solving
CPM framework 4Gs1, 4Gs2, 4Pt7; Teacher's Resource 14.1

3 Draw on the dotty paper with a ruler to make two of each of the shapes.

One shape must have no dots inside it and one must have at least 2 dots inside it.

Hint: The shapes could be regular or irregular. Lines can go vertically, horizontally or diagonally between the dots.

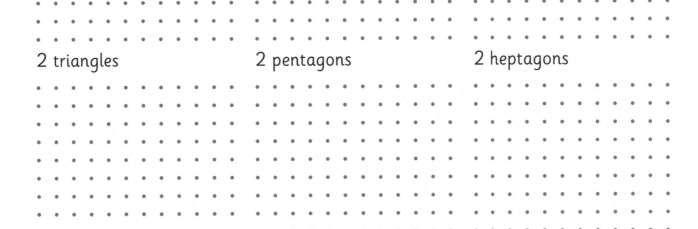

2 triangles   2 pentagons   2 heptagons

2 quadrilaterals   2 hexagons   2 octagons

4 Use a ruler to draw a shape in each of the sections of the Venn diagram.
The shape in the centre of the Venn diagram must be a quadrilateral with at least one line of symmetry and no right angles.

Hint: You could use a pegboard to explore the properties of different shapes before you draw them on the diagram.

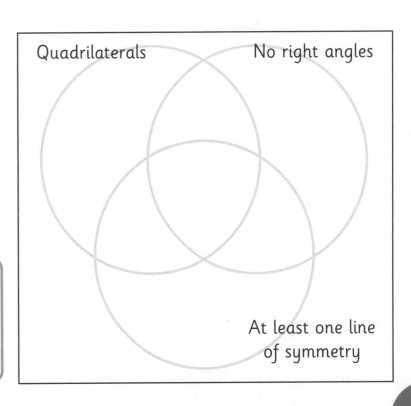

Quadrilaterals   No right angles

At least one line of symmetry

3D shapes

You will need:
thick paper or thin card, tracing paper, a ruler, scissors, sticky tape, resource 3, page 74, paper

Remember
To solve these problems you need to know some of the properties of pyramids, prisms and the tetrahedron. Use a mathematical dictionary to check definitions if you are unsure.

To make a 3D shape from a paper net, you must use a ruler to draw the net and your folds must be crisp and accurate.

Vocabulary
tetrahedron, tetrahedra (plural of tetrahedron), net, pyramid, prism

1   This is a regular heptagon.
    Use it as a template to help you make a net of a heptagonal prism.

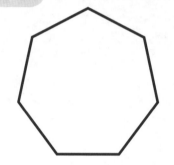

Copy the net onto thick paper or thin card.
Cut out and fold the net along each line to check that it makes a heptagonal prism.

Hint: A prism is a 3D shape with two identically shaped opposite faces, and all the other faces are rectangles.

Unit 2B: Geometry and problem solving
CPM framework 4Gs1, 4Gs4, 4Pt7; Teacher's Resource 14.2

2 Draw a net of a tetrahedron on the isometric dotty paper. Draw three more nets of tetrahedra; make them different sizes so that the tetraheda would fit inside each other.

Make the tetrahedra. Check that they fit inside each other.

Hint: For each tetrahedron, the triangular faces must be regular and identical.

3 Make a square-based pyramid with a height as close as you can to 8cm.

On a separate sheet of paper, describe how you made it.
Include sketches or photographs of the net and the model.

Hint: If you make the triangular faces of your pyramid 8 cm long the pyramid will be shorter than 8 cm because the faces have to lean in towards each other to join along the edges.
Do not try to calculate the sizes of the triangles. Make a square-based pyramid, measure its height and then try to improve the next net your draw.

Length

You will need: a ruler, a tape measure or metre stick, an unmarked straight edge, e.g. a strip of thick card

Remember

To measure with a ruler make sure that the start of the line or object lines up with the 0 position on the ruler.

1 m = 100 cm = 1000 mm

Vocabulary

metre, centimetre, millimetre

1   Use what you know about metres, centimetres and millimetres to complete this conversion table.

metres (m)	centimetres (cm)	millimetres (mm)
	100	
	200	
		5000
10		
20		

Hint: Remember how to multiply and divide by 10 and 100.

2   A long-course competition swimming pool must be 50 m long and have lanes that are 2.5 m wide. The pool must be a minimum of 1.35 m deep.

Convert the pool measurements into centimetres.

Length =

Lane width =

Depth =

Hint: Remember that 1 m = 100 cm.

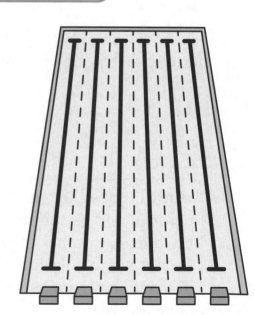

Unit 2C: Measure and problem solving
CPM framework 4Nn4, 4MI1, 4MI2, 4MI3, 4MI4, 4Pt2; Teacher's Resource 15.1

3 Use an unmarked straight edge to draw lines that you estimate are the lengths given below.

Use a ruler to measure the actual length of the lines. Record these lengths in centimetres, to the nearest millimetre, e.g. 4.6 cm.

A Draw a line that is approximately 5 cm long.

The line is actually ☐ long.

> **Hint:** Use the measured length of each line to help you estimate the length of the next line you draw.

B Draw a line that is approximately 10 cm long.

The line is actually ☐ long.

C Draw a line that is approximately 15 cm long.

The line is actually ☐ long.

4 This catalogue lists some objects for sale and their sizes. Some of the units of the measurement are wrong. Correct any that you think are wrong.

Item		Size
	Table lamp	30 m tall
	Kitchen table	90 mm high
	Washing machine	75 cm wide
	Vase	200 m tall
	Tablecloth	3 mm long
	Rug	2 m long

> **Hint:** You could look at a metre stick or a metre on a tape measure, and a centimetre and millimetre on a ruler, to help to visualise how long the measurement is in different units.

Talk to a partner or adult about why you think those units are wrong.

Time

Remember

To solve these problems you need to be able to find and use information in calendars and timetables. Look at the headings and make sure you know what information is being presented

When you are reading or recording the time, remember how both the hour hand and minute hand move around the clock face. The numbers around the edge of a standard clock indicate the hours.

You can draw a time line to help calculate with times. Remember that there are 60 minutes in 1 hour.

You will need: red and green coloured pencils or pens

Vocabulary
am (ante meridiem), pm (post meridiem), analogue clock, digital clock, calendar, date

1 Draw the time now on this analogue clock as accurately as possible.

How would this time look on a digital clock? ☐

These are the times Ewan saw on his watch during a soccer match.

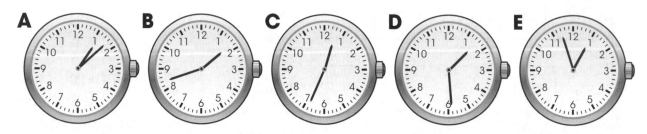

Write the letters in the boxes below, putting them in order from the earliest to the latest time.
Then write the times as digital clock times underneath.

How long was it between Ewan looking at his watch for the first time to the last time? ☐

Unit 1B: Measure and problem solving; Unit 2C: Measure and problem solving
CPM framework 4Dh1, 4Mt1, 4Mt2, 4Mt3, 4Mt4, 4Pt2; Teacher's Resource 5.2, 16.1, 16.2

Draw the time now on this clock as accurately as possible.

How would this time look on a digital clock?

How much time has passed between the time you recorded at the start of the activity and the next time you recorded?

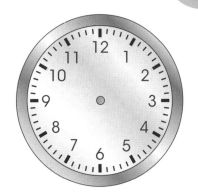

2   Parveen is catching a train to Porto. Complete the clock faces to show the times when there will be a train to Porto.

Departures			
Destination	**Platform**	**Departure time**	**Information**
Bonito	3	10:22 am	on time
Porto	2	10:49 am	12 minutes late
Tacuru	1	11:18 am	on time
Jussara	3	11:51 am	on time
Bonito	2	12:23 pm	18 minutes late
Porto	2	12:49 pm	on time
Alegre	2	1:15 pm	on time
Porto	3	1:24 pm	39 minutes late
Tacuru	2	1:57 pm	on time
Alegre	1	2:33 pm	on time

Danny is catching the train to Bonito.
This is the time on his watch.

How long does he have to wait for a train?

Unit 1B: Measure and problem solving; Unit 2C: Measure and problem solving
CPM framework 4Mt1, 4Mt2, 4Mt3, 4Mt4, 4Pt2; Teacher's Resource 5.2, 16.1, 16.2

49

3 This clock is not the correct way up.

Emily thinks it looks like a quarter past 6, but it is not.
Explain why the hands cannot be showing a quarter past 6.

What time is showing on the clock?
Write the hour numbers on the face.

Draw hands on this clock so that they make a
right angle and both hands are pointing
directly at numbers on the face.

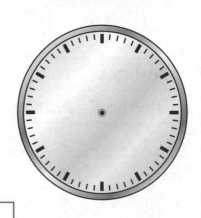

Which of these statements is true?
Write T or F in each box.

A   There are two times on the clock when
the hands make a right angle and at
least one hand is pointing at a number. ☐

B   There are four times on the clock when
the hands make a right angle and at
least one hand is pointing at a number. ☐

C   There are many times on the clock when
the hands make a right angle and at
least one hand is pointing at a number. ☐

Explain your answers.

Hint: Remember the hour hand is always moving slowly around the clock.
You could use an example or counter example to explain your reasoning.

Unit 1B: Measure and problem solving; Unit 2C: Measure and problem solving
CPM framework 4Mt1, 4Mt2, 4Mt3, 4Mt4, 4Pt2; Teacher's Resource 5.2, 16.1, 16.2

4 Find the route that takes the shortest amount of time.
Mark the route on the map, in green. The numbers are times, in minutes.

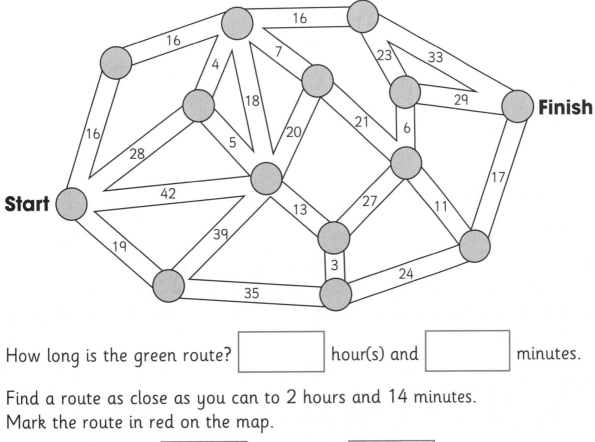

How long is the green route? ☐ hour(s) and ☐ minutes.

Find a route as close as you can to 2 hours and 14 minutes.
Mark the route in red on the map.

My red route takes ☐ hour(s) and ☐ minutes.

> **Hint:** You can convert minutes into hours or hours into minutes.
> There is a route that is exactly 2 hours and 14 minutes.

5 This is Abi's calendar. She is going to an art club on the
last Tuesday of each month for the rest of the year.
Can you work out the dates of the last Tuesday of each month?

> **Hint:** You will need to know how many days
> there are in each month of the year.

Unit 1B: Measure and problem solving; Unit 2C: Measure and problem solving
CPM framework 4Mt1, 4Mt2, 4Mt3, 4Mt4, 4Pt2; Teacher's Resource 5.2, 16.1, 16.2

51

Special numbers

Remember
To solve these problems you need to be able to recognise odd and even numbers. You can draw a number line with numbers lower than zero using negative numbers to help you solve problems involving negative and positive numbers.

You will need: a ruler

Vocabulary
positive, negative, odd, even

1 Write these number patterns.

Start on 7, count on in 9s.

What do you notice about the sum of the digits in each number in the pattern?

Start on 13, count on in 5s.

What do you notice about the pattern?

Start on –2, count on in 10s.

What do you notice about the pattern?

Start on –7, count on in 2s.

What do you notice about the pattern?

Unit 3A: Number and problem solving
CPM framework 4Nn14, 4Nn15, 4Nn16, 4Ps6; Teacher's Resource 18.1

2 Complete the addition and subtraction grids.

The sum of two even numbers is always even.

The difference between two even numbers is always even.

+	even	odd
even	even	
odd		

–	even	odd
even	even	
odd		

3 Look at the number patterns.
If you continued each pattern what would be the first number less than 0?

200, 190, 180, 170, ... ☐

39, 35, 31, 27, ... ☐

895, 795, 695, 595, ... ☐

4 Put this set of numbers in order, from lowest to highest value.
Describe the number pattern.

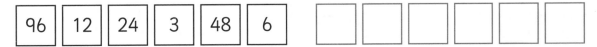

| 96 | 12 | 24 | 3 | 48 | 6 |

Put this set of numbers in order, from lowest to highest value.
Describe the number pattern.

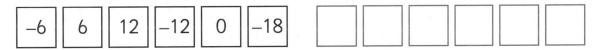

| –6 | 6 | 12 | –12 | 0 | –18 |

Suppose you continued the pattern. Do you think 121 would be in it? Why?

Fractions and division

1   Use these digits to make three mixed numbers. Position them on the number line.

| 2 | 3 | 4 |

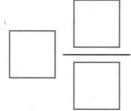   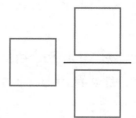

```
←——┼————————┼————————┼————————┼————————┼——→
   1        2        3        4        5
```

Unit 3A: Number and problem solving
CPM framework 4Nn17, 4Nn18, 4Nn19, 4Nn20, 4Nn21, 4Nn22, 4Nn23, 4Nn24, 4Nn25, 4Nc3; Teacher's Resource 19.1, 19.2, 19.3

2 Draw lines between two fractions to total 1.
Find all the pairs that total 1.

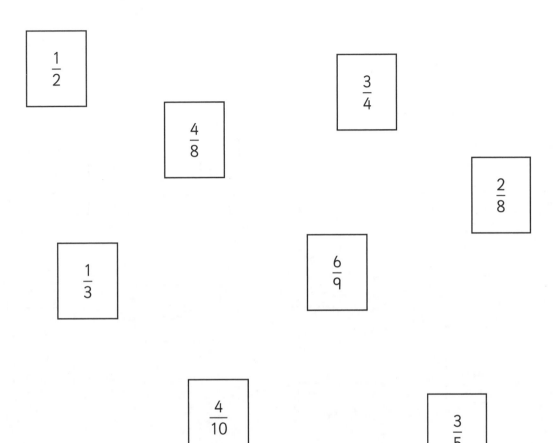

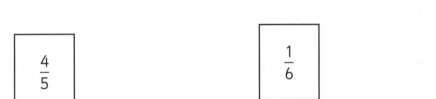

Hint: You will have to find equivalent fractions to make pairs that you recognise that total 1.

CPM framework 4Nn17, 4Nn18, 4Nn19, 4Nn20, 4Nn21, 4Nn22, 4Nn23, 4Nn24, 4Nn25, 4Nc3; Teacher's Resource 19.1, 19.2, 19.3

3 Draw lines to match each fraction to a decimal to total 1.

$\frac{1}{2}$

0.25

$\frac{1}{4}$

$\frac{3}{4}$

0.5

0.75

0.7

$\frac{3}{10}$

0.2

0.1

$\frac{8}{10}$

0.8

$\frac{6}{10}$

$\frac{9}{10}$

0.4

95/100

92/100

0.05

99/100

0.01

4 Shade $\frac{1}{4}$ of the grid red.

Shade $\frac{1}{3}$ of the grid blue.

Shade $\frac{1}{6}$ of the grid yellow.

What fraction of the grid is unshaded?

Unit 3A: Number and problem solving
CPM framework 4Nn17, 4Nn18, 4Nn19, 4Nn20, 4Nn21, 4Nn22, 4Nn23, 4Nn24, 4Nn25, 4Nc3; Teacher's Resource 19.1, 19.2, 19.3

5 Which is greater, $\frac{2}{3}$ or $\frac{7}{9}$?

That would be [ ] silver coins.

18 silver coins

Which is greater, $\frac{5}{8}$ or $\frac{3}{4}$?

That would be [ ] silver coins.

24 silver coins

Which is greater, $\frac{3}{5}$ or $\frac{7}{10}$?

That would be [ ] silver coins.

40 silver coins

Place these fractions on the number line as accurately as you can.

| $\frac{2}{3}$ | $\frac{7}{9}$ | $\frac{5}{8}$ | $\frac{3}{4}$ | $\frac{3}{5}$ | $\frac{7}{10}$ |

0 ———————————————————————————————→ 1

Hint: Use equivalence to help you order the fractions on the number line.

Ratio and proportion

Remember

You can use **in every** to compare the size of one part to the whole set. For example, in every packet of 7 sweets there are 2 strawberry sweets.

You can use **for every** to compare the size of two parts of a set. For example, for every 2 strawberry sweets there are 3 lime sweets.

You will need: red, blue and yellow coloured pencils

Vocabulary

in every, for every

1 Design a matching necklace and bracelet. Use red, yellow and blue beads.

Follow both of these instructions for the colours of the beads.

- In every 6 beads, 3 are blue.

- For every 2 yellow beads there is 1 red bead.

Complete the table to show how many beads of each colour there are on the bracelet and necklace.

	Number of blue beads	Number of red beads	Number of yellow beads
bracelet			
necklace			

Hint: First count how many beads there are in the bracelet and in the necklace.

Unit 3A: Number and problem solving
CPM framework 4Nc26; Teacher's Resource 20.1

2 Klara and Aramide have been collecting star and planet stickers for their walls.

Klara's stickers

In every ☐ sticker(s), ☐ are star(s).

For every ☐ star(s) there are ☐ planet(s).

Aramide's stickers

In every ☐ sticker(s), ☐ are star(s).

For every ☐ star(s) there are ☐ planet(s).

Klara and Aramide put their stickers together. Write two sentences about the whole set of stickers using 'in every' and 'for every'.

3 Sanjay is mixing a drink using 100 ml apple juice, 90 ml orange juice and 60 ml cranberry juice. This makes enough for one person.

How much of each juice would he need to make enough for 8 people? ☐ ☐ ☐

What is the total volume of juice needed for 8 people, in litres? ☐

Unit 3A: Number and problem solving
CPM framework 4Nc26; Teacher's Resource 20.1

Capacity

Remember

There are 1000 millilitres in 1 litre. You can use this to work out how many millilitres are in 2 litres, and how many millilitres are in $\frac{1}{2}$ litre.

You can use a place-value chart to help you understand measures given in litres with decimal parts.

Vocabulary
litre (l), millilitre (ml)

You will need:
coloured pencils,
a place-value chart

1 Shade in the measuring bottle. Use these colours.

0 to 0.5 litres in red.

0.5 to 0.7 litres in green.

0.7 to 1.2 litres in blue.

1.2 to 1.8 litres in yellow.

Hint: Work out the size of the divisions on the scale. You could label the scale with the missing numbers.

Unit 3B: Measure and problem solving
CPM framework 4MI1, 4MI2, 4MI3, 4MI4, 4Pt2; Teacher's Resource 21.1

2 There should be $2\frac{1}{2}$ litres of oil in each can.

Estimate how many millilitres of oil are needed to fill each can.

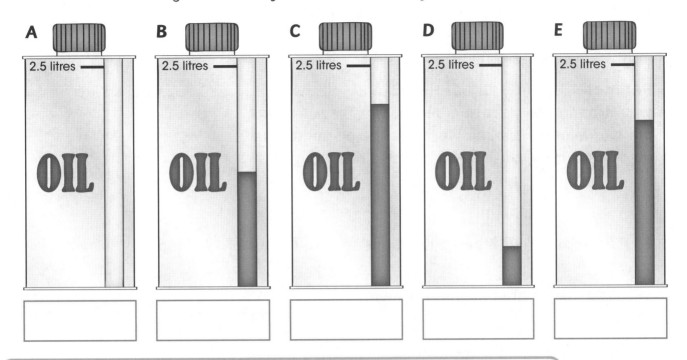

Hint: You could use a ruler to mark some divisions onto the oil cans.

3 Aziz is going to make a five-tier cake.

Each cake needs half the amount of cake batter than the cake beneath it. The first tin uses 1 litre of batter. How much batter goes into the fifth tin? Round your answer to the nearest 10 ml.

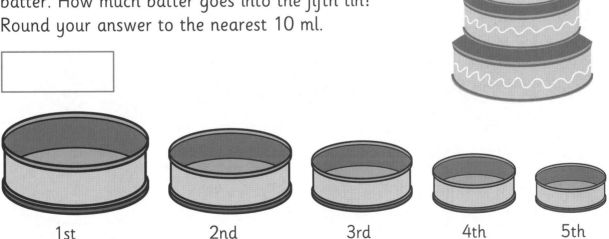

Hint: You will need to work out how much is needed for each tin. Work out your answers in millilitres rather than litres.

Area and perimeter

Remember

Area is a measure of the surface covered by a shape. It is measured in square units. You can work out the area by seeing how many squares it covers.

Perimeter is a measure of the distance all the way around the sides of a shape. It is measured in units of length. You can work out the perimeter by measuring all of the sides then calculating the total.

You will need:
resource 4, page 75, tracing paper, an unmarked straight edge, a ruler

Vocabulary
area, perimeter, square centimetre, cm^2

---

1 Use resource 4. Make a rectangle that is 7 rows of 16 squares.

What is the area of the rectangle?

What is the perimeter of the rectangle?

Fold the rectangle in half so that it is 7 rows of 8 squares.

What is the area of the rectangle?

What is the perimeter of the rectangle?

Predict what the area and perimeter of the rectangle would be if you folded it in half again.

Area =

Perimeter =

Check your answers by folding the rectangle in half so that it is 7 rows of 4 squares.

Hint: Remember to use cm^2 units for area and cm units for perimeter.

Unit 3B: Measure and problem solving
CPM framework 4Ma1, 4Ma2, 4Ma3, 4Pt2; Teacher's Resource 23.1

2 Estimate the area and perimeter of each shape.

Then trace the shapes and lay the traced shapes over the centimetre-squared paper to find out the actual area and perimeter of each shape.

> **Hint:** If you have a finger that is approximately 1 cm wide you could place it on the shapes to help you estimate the perimeter and area.

Shape A

Estimated area

Estimated perimeter

Actual area

Actual perimeter

Shape C

Estimated area

Estimated perimeter

Actual area

Actual perimeter

Shape B

Estimated area

Estimated perimeter

Actual area

Actual perimeter

Shape D

Estimated area

Estimated perimeter

Actual area

Actual perimeter

3 Use an unmarked straight edge, such as the edge of a piece of card, to draw a rectangle without measuring the sides.

Measure the sides to the nearest centimetre and calculate the perimeter.

cm

Make and measure more rectangles in the same way.
Label each rectangle with the lengths of the sides and the perimeter.
Try to get as close as you can to a perimeter of 18 cm.

Hint: You could make and use a right-angle checker to ensure that the corners of the rectangles you draw are 90°.

Unit 3B: Measure and problem solving
CPM framework 4Ma1, 4Ma2, 4Ma3, 4Pt2; Teacher's Resource 23.1

Graphs, tables, diagrams and charts

Remember

To solve these problems you need to know that information can be displayed in different ways. Some of these ways are clearer than others for communicating the information.

Draw graphs with a ruler, and make sure that bars on a bar graph are all the same width.

You will need: a ruler

Vocabulary
frequency table, tally chart, tree diagram, branching database, bar chart, Carroll diagram, Venn diagram

---

1 Complete the frequency table below, showing flavours of lollies bought.

Ice lollies bought today		
Flavour	**Tally**	**Total**
Strawberry	ЖЖ ЖЖ ЖЖ III	
Watermelon	ЖЖ ЖЖ III	
Pineapple	ЖЖ ЖЖ ЖЖ ЖЖ IIII	
Blackcurrant		15
Mango		17

Show the frequency table information on both bar graphs.

Which bar graph do you think shows the information more clearly? Why?

Ice lollies bought today

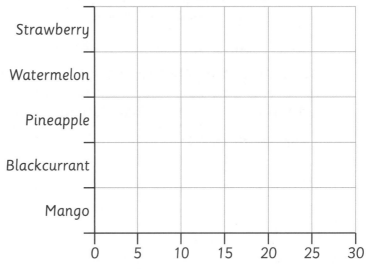

Ice lollies bought today

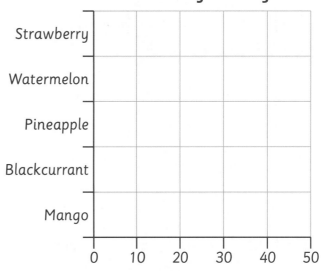

Unit 3C: Handling data and problem solving
CPM framework 4Dh1, 4Dh2, 4Dh3, 4Ps4; Teacher's Resource 24.1, 24.2, 25.1, 25.2

65

2 This bar graph shows the average temperatures at Cambridge Bay, Canada in Celsius degrees (°C).

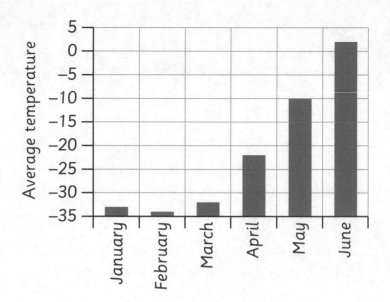

What was the temperature in May? ☐ °C

What is the highest average temperature? ☐ °C

What is the lowest average temperature? ☐ °C

This is a table with temperatures for the next 6 months.
Label and complete the graph with the information from the table.

Month	July	August	September	October	November	December
Temperature (°C)	8	6	−1	−12	−24	−30

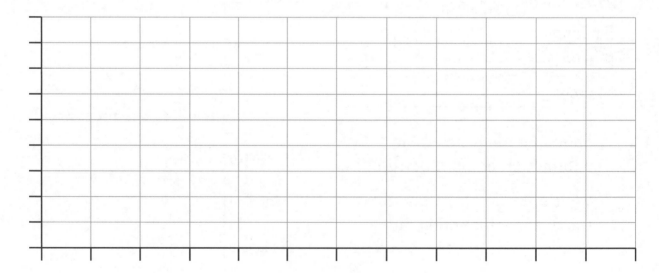

Hint: Look at the numbers that need to be recorded and choose a scale to fit.

Unit 3C: Handling data and problem solving
CPM framework 4Dh1, 4Dh2, 4Dh3, 4Ps4; Teacher's Resource 24.1, 24.2, 25.1, 25.2

3 Use this tree diagram to sort a set of numbers. You could use
18, –24, 27, 19, 14, –21, –5, –14, or choose numbers of your own.

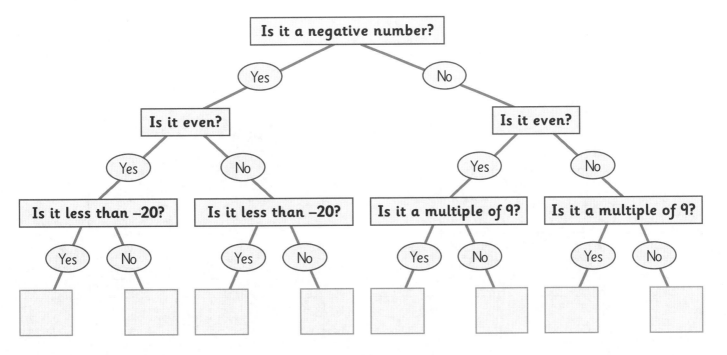

Sort the numbers you have put at the end of the
branches of the tree diagram into this Venn diagram.

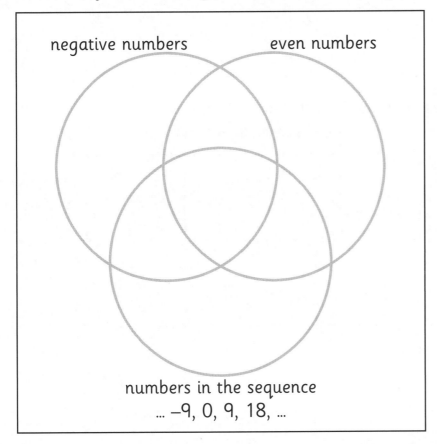

> **Hint:** Write numbers
> that are not negative,
> not even and not in the
> number sequence in the
> section of the diagram
> outside the rings.

Unit 3C: Handling data and problem solving
CPM framework 4Dh1, 4Dh2, 4Dh3, 4Ps4; Teacher's Resource 24.1, 24.2, 25.1, 25.2

67

4 Write your own questions that will help someone to sort numbers. Write one number at the end of each branch of the diagram.

Hint: You can ask questions such as:
Is it odd?
Is it > 8?

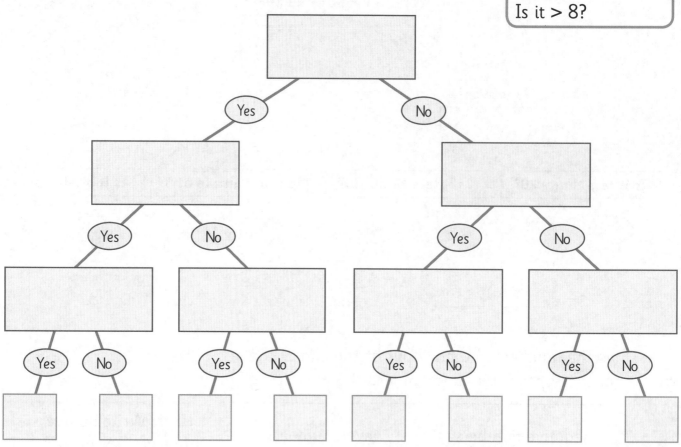

Make a Carroll diagram that will sort the same numbers so that there is at least one of the numbers in each section.

Unit 3C: Handling data and problem solving
CPM framework 4Dh1, 4Dh2, 4Dh3, 4Ps4; Teacher's Resource 24.1, 24.2, 25.1, 25.2

Problems and puzzles

Remember

You need to understand the position of digits in a number is important to its value. Some of the positions are thousands, hundreds, tens, ones.

Use ordered lists and tables to help you solve problems systematically.

To solve problems using logic use sentences such as 'If this is true, then this must also be true', or 'If this is true, then this must not be true'.

You will need:
counters

Vocabulary
logic, systematically

1   This is an abacus. Beads are put onto the rods to make numbers.

This number is 1461.

There are only 12 beads.

If you use every bead:

(a) what is the lowest number that can be made on the abacus?

(b) what is the highest number that can be made?

(c) 2345 cannot be made with these beads on the abacus. Explain why.

(d) There are 412 possible numbers that can be made using all of the beads and the abacus. How many can you find?

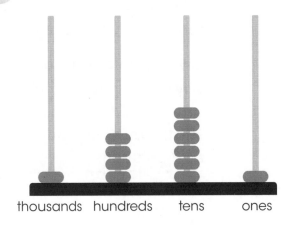

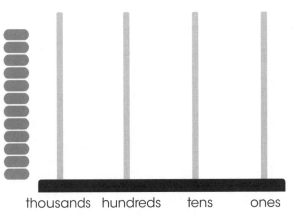

Hint: You can use 12 counters on the picture to make some numbers first. Work systematically to find all of the possibilities.

Unit 3C: Handling data and problem solving
CPM framework 4Dh1, 4Dh2, 4Dh3, 4Ps4, 4Ps5, 4Ps6; Teacher's Resource 24.1, 24.2, 25.1, 25.2

2 24 litres of soda need to be packaged in 2 litre bottles.

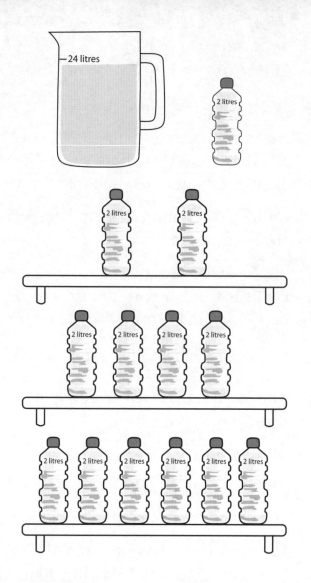

The 2 litre bottles will be arranged on 3 shelves in the shop.

There must be a different number of bottles on each shelf.

There must be more bottles on the bottom shelf than on any other shelf.

There must be the least number of bottles on the top shelf.

How many litres of soda could be on each shelf? Find all the possibilities.

Hint: Work systematically to find all 7 solutions.

3 Each shape in the grid represents a number. Complete the grid.

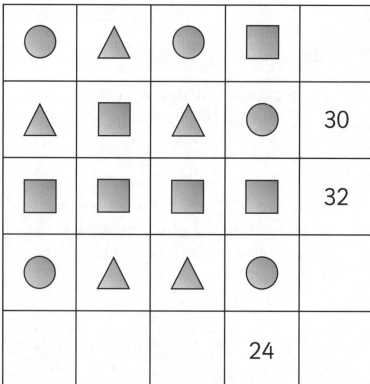

Hint: You could start by working out what number is represented by ▢.

Unit 3C: Handling data and problem solving
CPM framework 4Dh1, 4Dh2, 4Dh3, 4Ps4, 4Ps5, 4Ps6; Teacher's Resource 24.1, 24.2, 25.1, 25.2

4 Staff at an art gallery are interested in knowing about the people visiting the gallery, and which rooms in the gallery the visitors prefer.

> **Hint:** Use the information in the clues to help you calculate the missing numbers.

This is the information they have found out:

- 52 adults visited the gallery in total.
- 10 of the adults preferred room 4.
- 14 of the children preferred room 2.
- A different number of adults and children visited the gallery.
- There was a total of 114 visitors.
- Twice as many children preferred room 2 to room 4.
- Half as many adults preferred room 1 to room 2.
- 30 visitors in total preferred room 2.
- The same number of children as adults preferred room 3.

Use the information to complete the table.

Preferred room		Adults	Children	Total
	Room 1			
	Room 2			
	Room 3			
	Room 4			
Total				

5 Bibi is learning to knit. Each day she gets quicker, and is able to knit one more row than the day before.

- On Sunday she knitted 1 row.
- On Monday she knitted 2 rows.
- On Tuesday she knitted 3 rows...

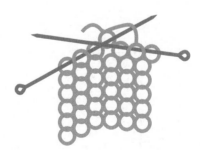

Bibi is knitting a scarf that must be at least 250 rows long.

How many days will it take Bibi to knit the scarf?

> **Hint:** Write down the total number of rows that have been knitted after each day.

Unit 3C: Handling data and problem solving
CPM framework 4Dh1, 4Dh2, 4Dh3, 4Ps4, 4Ps5, 4Ps6; Teacher's Resource 24.1, 24.2, 25.1, 25.2

71

Resource 1
Place-value chart and Carroll diagram

Place-value chart

1000	2000	3000	4000	5000	6000	7000	8000	9000
100	200	300	400	500	600	700	800	900
10	20	30	40	50	60	70	80	90
1	2	3	4	5	6	7	8	9
0.1	0.2	0.3	0.4	0.5	0.6	0.7	0.8	0.9
0.01	0.02	0.03	0.04	0.05	0.06	0.07	0.08	0.09

Carroll diagram

	Multiple of 4	Not a multiple of 4
Multiple of 3		
Not a multiple of 3		

Photocopiable resources

Original material © Cambridge University Press 2016

1	2	3	4	5
6	7	8	9	10
11	12	13	14	15
16	17	18	19	20
21	22	23	24	25
26	27	28	29	30

Resource 3
Isometric dotted paper

Photocopiable resources

Answers

Page 4 Numbers and the number system

1 ON

2

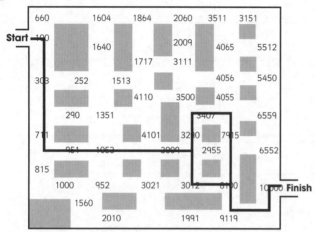

3 811, 908, 1000, 1091, 1810, 8001, 8999, 9080
Word: symmetry

4 9177 (nine thousand, one hundred and seventy-seven)

5 Game

6 Possible solutions are 1919, 1937, 1955, 1973, 1991.

Page 8 Addition and subtraction

1 10, 14, 18, 22, 26, 30, 34, 38, 42, 46, 50, 54, 58, 62, 66, 70, 74, 78.

2 Bella 65, Alyssa 27, Tanya 38, Sara 29, Kim 48

3 Route that totals 200 goes through 10, 12, 37, 69, 45 and 27.

4 Game

5

Name	Week one (ml)	Week two (ml)	Total
Abigail	476	764	1240
Maria	816	396	1212
Kyle	519	229	748
Oshi	383	459	842
Lila	410	649	1059
Rani	825	243	1068

The difference between Kyle's and Oshi's totals is 94 ml.

6 There is more than one solution.
One possible solution:
987 − 654 = 333
975 − 864 = 111
759 − 486 = 273
759 − 684 = 75
569 − 478 = 91
795 − 468 = 327
846 − 759 = 87
864 − 795 = 69

Page 12 Multiplication and division

1 Yousef has earned $403. Naser has earned $395

2

×	9	10	2	7	4	5	3	6	8	1
9	81	90	18	63	36	45	27	54	72	9
10	90	100	20	70	40	50	30	60	80	10
2	18	20	4	14	8	10	6	12	16	2
7	63	70	14	49	28	35	21	42	56	7
4	36	40	8	28	16	20	12	24	32	4
5	45	50	10	35	20	25	15	30	40	5
3	27	30	6	21	12	15	9	18	24	3
6	54	60	12	42	24	30	18	36	48	6
8	72	80	16	56	32	40	24	48	64	8
1	9	10	2	7	4	5	3	6	8	1

3 27, 54, 81, 108, 135, 162, 189, 216, 243, 270
The children might notice that the sequence is 'odd, even, odd, even ...'. They might notice that for all of the multiples, except 189, the digits of each number total 9 (the digits of 189 add up to 18, then the digits of 18 total 9).

4 42 × 2 = 84, 28 × 3 = 84, 21 × 4 = 84, 14 × 6 = 84, 12 × 7 = 84.

5 The route to the celebration starts from C

6 Numbers that cannot be made are 1, 5, 10, 11, 15 and 20, either because a digit would need to be used twice or a 0 is required. There are many solutions for the other numbers.

Page 17 Weight

1 G, A, D, B, F, E, C, H
Scale should be labelled approximately: A 630 g, B 1 kg 10 g, C 1 kg 360 g, D 950 g, E 1 kg 170 g, F 1040 g, G 190 g, H 1980 g

2 Children's own answers

3 Answers based on estimations of 100 g, 200 g, 400 g and 800 g.

4 The piles could be:
15 kg 800 g = 4900 g + 7200 g + 3700 g
15 kg 950 g = 3100 g + 8900 g + 3950 g

5 Cone = 500 g, cube = 300 g, sphere = 100 g
Scale should indicate 2 kg 200 g

6 Various possible answers depending on child's explanation.

Page 20 Pictograms

1 Animation
Action
20 people

Film genre	Number of people
Action	50
Comedy	95
Animation	120
Documentary	65

2

Leo	★ ★ ★ ★ ★ ★ ★ ◗
Bruno	★ ★ ★ ★ ★ ★ ★ ◖
Jamil	★ ★ ★ ★ ★ ◗
Vijay	★ ★ ★ ★ ★ ★ ★ ◖

The positions of Bruno and Vijay's rows in the pictogram can be reversed.

3 The pictogram should match the data in the table using a suitable scale (not 1 symbol for 1 flight). There should be axes labels and a key.

Page 22 Carroll and Venn diagrams

1 There is more than one solution. Here is one possible solution:
6 + 3 = 9
7 − 5 = 2
4 × 9 = 36
8 ÷ 2 = 4

2

	Hat	No hat
Tie	Archie	Adam
No tie	Amos	Albert

3 Flowers in the Venn diagram should match the category labels.

4 3

Page 24 Place value and decimals in context

1 Ali, Aadi

2 7325, 4013

3 Shaded grid reveals the word TIP

4 Maria: $6.50, Caleb: $4.79, Tansy: $7.94, Ahmed: $9.75, Josie: $5.50

5 Samir $9.08, Greta $9.80, Lila $8.99.
Lila collected the least money, Greta collected most.

6 Amounts should be arranged in this order on the number line:
$0.06, 27 cents, $0.50, 62 cents, $0.81, $1, $1.08, 118 cents, $1.32, 150 cents, $1.88, $1.95.

Page 28 Odd, even and negative numbers

1 There are many solutions. Two solutions are:
−17 < −13 < −4 < −3, 12 > 7 > 5
−3 < 5 < 7 < 12, −4 > −13 > −17
−17 and −13 cannot go in the box marked with the star.

2 The word is 'icicles'.

3 Path D leads to the goal.

4 No. One way to explain why the game is not fair is that the highest possible spin for evens is 10 and for odds is only 9. The lowest possible spin for evens is 2, but for odds it is 1.
The second is their game board. It is the only one with the Evens player on an even number. The Evens player only adds on even numbers so the total will always be even.

5 Even, odd, even, even, even, odd.

Page 32 Addition, subtraction, multiplication and division

1 605 + 197 = 802, 901 − 605 = 296

2 Game: 389, 388, 299, 288

3 3 × 21 = 63, 5 × 46 = 230, 7 × 98 = 686

4 There is more than one solution.
97 ÷ **2** = **48** remainder 1, 97 ÷ **5** = **19** remainder 2
97 ÷ **7** = **13** remainder 6, 97 ÷ **9** = **10** remainder 7
The numbers that leave a remainder 1 are 2, 3, 4, 6 and 8.

5 9, 18, 27, 36, 45, 54, 63, 72, 81, 90
These are the first 10 multiples of 9.
The pattern starts on 9 and counts on 9.

6 32, 46, 43, 59

Page 36 Angles, position and direction

1 12, 16, 28, 32

2 Octagon

3 D, A, E, C, B, F

4 Kim started from (C, 1)

5 Tom started from (B, 7).

Page 40 Symmetry

1

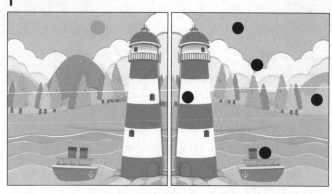

2 Check that the shapes the learner has stuck into the table have the correct number of lines of symmetry.

3 One vertical line of symmetry, one horizontal line of symmetry, one diagonal line of symmetry, one diagonal line of symmetry (opposite diagonal to the previous tile); 5 lines of symmetry

4 (3, 5), (4, 5), (5, 5), (6, 5), (3, 6), (4, 6), (5, 6), (6, 6)
Solutions do not need to be listed in this order.

Page 42 2D shapes

1 A, D, E

2 Shape 1 is a rectangle, shape 2 is a square, shape 3 is a heptagon.

3 There are many solutions. Two of each shape should be drawn in each dotted grid. One should have no dots inside it, one should have at least two dots inside it.

4 8 shapes should be drawn in the Venn diagram that match the labels.

Page 44 3D shapes

1 The net should comprise two heptagons and seven rectangular faces. The heptagons should not share an edge.

2 Children should have drawn 4 nets of tetrahedra of different sizes.

3 Children should have described how they made their square-based pyramid as close to 8 cm tall as they could. They should include sketches or photographs of the net and model.

Page 46 Length

1

metres (m)	centimetres (cm)	millimetres (mm)
1	100	1000
2	200	2000
5	500	5000
10	1000	10 000
20	2000	20 000

2 5000 cm, 250 cm, 135 cm

3 Measure to check that the measurements accurately match the length of the lines drawn.

4

Item	Size
Table lamp	30 ~~m~~ cm tall
Kitchen table	90 ~~mm~~ cm high
Washing machine	75 cm wide
Vase	200 ~~m~~ mm tall
Tablecloth	3 ~~mm~~ m long
Rug	2 m long

Page 48 Time

1 C, E, A, D, B
12:34, 12:57, 1:08, 1:29, 1:42;
1 hour and 8 minutes

2 Clocks showing 11:01, 12:49 and 2:03; 46 minutes

3 3 o'clock
A is correct. If the hour hand is pointing directly at a number it must be an o'clock time, the only o'clock times when the hands are at right angles are 3 o'clock and 9 o'clock. If the minute hand is pointing directly to a number then to make a right angle the hour hand must also be pointing directly to a number.

4 The shortest route (green) takes 1 hour and 21 minutes

The 2 hours and 14 minutes route goes through 19 + 39 + 20 + 21 + 6 + 29

5 31 May, 28 June, 26 July, 30 August, 27 September, 25 October, 29 November, 27 December

Page 52 Special numbers

1 7, 16, 25, 34, 43, 52, 61, 70
The numbers are alternately odd and even.
All of the numbers have a digit sum of 7.
13, 18, 23, 28, 33, 38, 43, 48
The ones digit is always 3 or 8.
−2, 8, 18, 28, 38, 48, 58, 68
All of the numbers are even.
The ones digit is always 8, except for −2.
−7, −5, −3, −1, 1, 3, 5, 7
All of the numbers are odd.

2

+	even	odd
even	even	odd
odd	odd	even

−	even	odd
even	even	odd
odd	odd	even

3 −10, −1, −5

4 Each number is double the number before.
The numbers count on in 6s; they are multiples of 6.
121 would not be in the pattern because it is odd and 6, which is even, is repeatedly added onto the even numbers in the pattern so the terms will always be even.

Page 54 Fractions and division

1 $2\frac{3}{4}$, $3\frac{2}{4}$, $4\frac{2}{3}$

2 $\frac{1}{2}$ and $\frac{4}{8}$, $\frac{3}{4}$ and $\frac{2}{8}$, $\frac{1}{3}$ and $\frac{6}{9}$, $\frac{3}{5}$ and $\frac{4}{10}$, $\frac{4}{5}$ and $\frac{2}{10}$, $\frac{1}{6}$ and $\frac{10}{12}$

3 $\frac{1}{2}$ and 0.5, 0.25 and $\frac{3}{4}$, 0.75 and $\frac{1}{4}$, 0.2 and $\frac{8}{10}$, 0.7 and $\frac{3}{10}$, $\frac{9}{10}$ and 0.1, 0.4 and $\frac{6}{10}$, $\frac{95}{100}$ and 0.05, $\frac{99}{100}$ and 0.01, $\frac{92}{100}$ and 0.08

4 $\frac{1}{4}$

5 $\frac{7}{9}$, 14 silver coins; $\frac{3}{4}$, 18 silver coins; $\frac{7}{10}$, 28 silver coins

Page 58 Ratio and proportion

1

	Number of blue beads	Number of red beads	Number of yellow beads
bracelet	6	2	4
necklace	15	5	10

2 In every 3 stickers, 2 are stars.
For every 2 stars there is 1 planet.
In every 5 stickers, there are 3 stars.
For every 3 stars there are 2 planets.
More than one solution, e.g:
In every 44 stickers there are 16 planets.
For every 16 planets there are 28 stars

3 800 ml apple juice, 720 ml orange juice, 480 ml cranberry juice; 2 litres

Page 60 Capacity

1 Children will have shaded sections of the bottle using the scale:
0 to 0.5 litres in red, 0.5 to 0.7 litres in green, 0.7 to 1.2 litres in blue, 1.2 to 1.8 litres in yellow.

2 A = 2500 ml
B = a good estimate should be approximately 1250 ml
C = a good estimate should be between 100 ml and 300 ml
D = a good estimate should be between 2300 ml and 2400 ml
E = a good estimate should be between 500 ml and 750 ml

3 60 ml

Page 62 Area and perimeter

1 112 cm², 46 cm; 56 cm², 30 cm; 28 cm², 22 cm

2 Actual areas and perimeters are:
12 cm², 16 cm; 12 cm², 14 cm; 28 cm², 22 cm; 9 cm², 20 cm

3 Children's own answers.

Page 65 Graphs, tables, diagrams and charts

1 18, 13, 24, ⅢⅢⅢ, ⅢⅢⅢ ll

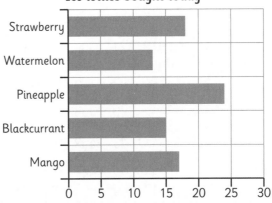

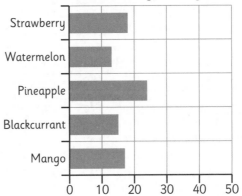

The first graph shows the data more clearly.

2 −10°C, 2°C, −34°C
The temperatures represented in the graph should match the temperatures in the table.

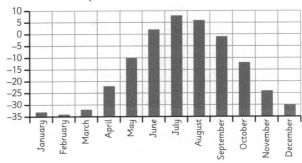

3 Check that children's numbers are sorted correctly in their branching database and their Venn diagram.

4 Check that children's numbers are sorted correctly in their branching database and their Carroll diagram.

1 (a) 39

(b) 9300

(c) 2345 cannot be made because it would require 14 beads.

(d) All possible numbers:

39, 48, 57, 66, 129, 138, 147, 156, 165, 174, 183, 192, 219, 228, 237, 246, 255, 264, 273, 282, 291, 309, 318, 327, 336, 345, 354, 363, 372, 381, 390, 408, 417, 426, 435, 444, 453, 462, 471, 480, 507, 516, 525, 534, 543, 552, 561, 570, 606, 615, 624, 633, 642, 651, 660, 705, 714, 723, 732, 741, 750, 804, 813, 822, 831, 840, 903, 912, 921, 930, 1029, 1038, 1047, 1056, 1065, 1074, 1083, 1092, 1119, 1128, 1137, 1146, 1155, 1164, 1173, 1182, 1191, 1209, 1218, 1227, 1236, 1245, 1254, 1263, 1272, 1281, 1290, 1308, 1317, 1326, 1335, 1344, 1353, 1362, 1371, 1380, 1407, 1416, 1425, 1434, 1443, 1452, 1461, 1470, 1506, 1515, 1524, 1533, 1542, 1551, 1560, 1605, 1614, 1623, 1632, 1641, 1650, 1704, 1713, 1722, 1731, 1740, 1803, 1812, 1821, 1830, 1902, 1911, 1920, 2019, 2028, 2037, 2046, 2055, 2064, 2073, 2082, 2091, 2109, 2118, 2127, 2136, 2145, 2154, 2163, 2172, 2181, 2190, 2208, 2217, 2226, 2235, 2244, 2253, 2262, 2271, 2280, 2307, 2316, 2325, 2334, 2343, 2352, 2361, 2370, 2406, 2415, 2424, 2433, 2442, 2451, 2460, 2505, 2514, 2523, 2532, 2541, 2550, 2604, 2613, 2622, 2631, 2640, 2703, 2712, 2721, 2730, 2802, 2811, 2820, 2901, 2910, 3009, 3018, 3027, 3036, 3045, 3054, 3063, 3072, 3081, 3090, 3108, 3117, 3126, 3135, 3144, 3153, 3162, 3171, 3180, 3207, 3216, 3225, 3234, 3243, 3252, 3261, 3270, 3306, 3315, 3324, 3333, 3342, 3351, 3360, 3405, 3414, 3423, 3432, 3441, 3450, 3504, 3513, 3522, 3531, 3540, 3603, 3612, 3621, 3630, 3702, 3711, 3720, 3801, 3810, 3900, 4008, 4017, 4026, 4035, 4044, 4053, 4062, 4071, 4080, 4107, 4116, 4125, 4134, 4143, 4152, 4161, 4170, 4206, 4215, 4224, 4233, 4242, 4251, 4260, 4305, 4314, 4323, 4332, 4341, 4350, 4404, 4413, 4422, 4431, 4440, 4503, 4512, 4521, 4530, 4602, 4611, 4620, 4701, 4710, 4800, 5007, 5016, 5025, 5034, 5043, 5052, 5061, 5070, 5106, 5115, 5124, 5133, 5142, 5151, 5160, 5205, 5214, 5223, 5232, 5241, 5250, 5304, 5313, 5322, 5331, 5340, 5403, 5412, 5421, 5430, 5502, 5511, 5520, 5601, 5610, 5700, 6006, 6015, 6024, 6033, 6042, 6051, 6060, 6105, 6114, 6123, 6132, 6141, 6150, 6204, 6213, 6222, 6231, 6240, 6303, 6312, 6321, 6330, 6402, 6411, 6420, 6501, 6510, 6600, 7005, 7014, 7023, 7032, 7041, 7050, 7104, 7113, 7122, 7131, 7140, 7203, 7212, 7221, 7230, 7302, 7311, 7320, 7401, 7410, 7500, 8004, 8013, 8022, 8031, 8040, 8103, 8112, 8121, 8130, 8202, 8211, 8220, 8301, 8310, 8400, 9003, 9012, 9021, 9030, 9102, 9111, 9120, 9201, 9210, 9300.

2 2 litres, 4 litres, 18 litres

2 litres, 6 litres, 16 litres

2 litres, 8 litres, 14 litres

2 litres, 10 litres, 12 litres

4 litres, 6 litres, 14 litres

4 litres, 8 litres, 12 litres

6 litres, 8 litres, 10 litres.

3

○	△	○	■	25
△	■	△	○	30
■	■	■	■	32
○	△	△	○	26
25	34	30	24	

4

		Adults	Children	Total
Preferred room	Room 1	8	23	31
	Room 2	16	14	30
	Room 3	18	18	36
	Room 4	10	7	17
	Total	52	62	114

5 22 days